LIKE A LASTING STORM: HELPING WITH REAL-LIFE PROBLEMS

Cooper B. Holmes
Emporia State University

CLINICAL PSYCHOLOGY PUBLISHING CO., INC.
4 CONANT SQUARE
BRANDON, VT 05733

LIKE A LASTING STORM:
HELPING WITH
REAL-LIFE PROBLEMS

Library of Congress Cataloging-in-Publication Data
Like a lasting storm: helping with real-life problems / Cooper B. Holmes.
      p. cm.
  Includes bibliographical references and index.
  ISBN 0-88422-124-5
  1. Life change events. 2. Stress (Psychology). 3. Mental health counseling.
I. Title
RC455.4.L53H65   1994
616.89—dc20   94-10224
                                             CIP

Library of Congress Catalog Card Number: 94-10224
ISBN: 0-88422-124-5

 4 Conant Square
Brandon, Vermont 05733

Cover Design: Thomas Hannan

Printed in the United States of America

This book is dedicated to
Bick and Martha, Darl and Dody, and Carman.
And, to Ashley and Andrew's friend,
"Hooch" Froelich.

TABLE OF CONTENTS

PREFACE

In an ideal world, people would always benefit from a difficult situation and turn it to some personal gain. However, to categorically assume that a person will emerge renewed from a crisis is naive and ignores the reality of what life crises can do to a person. I do not believe that every life crisis offers a challenge or an opportunity for positive growth experience, a chance to emerge a better and stronger person. In the real world, an event may leave a person changed in ways that could only be construed as adverse. A person's failure to gain strength from such an event reflects the reality of personal experience, not some problem in the attitude or perspective of the person. As the title of this book indicates, for some people, life becomes "like a lasting storm." Rynearson (1981), a psychiatrist writing about the suicide of his wife, wrote:

> Finally, it is important for the survivor to recognize that in spite of time and introspection, this experience will always remain a complex nidus. I and other survivors can never be "cured" in the sense of being restored, for suicide represents a life change that literally "changes one" (p. 86).

The phrase "like a lasting storm" comes from Shakespeare's *Pericles, Prince of Tyre* (1982), in which Marina exclaims upon the news of the death of her nurse:

> No, I will rob Tellus of her weed,
> To strew thy green with flowers. The yellows, blues,

> The purple violets, and marigolds
> Shall as a carpet hang upon thy grave
> While summer days do last. Ay me! Poor maid,
> Born in a tempest, when my mother died,
> This world to me is like a lasting storm,
> Whirring me from my friends. (p. 1012)

This quotation yields a suitable title for this book for two reasons. First, it captures the essence of the struggle life becomes for some people. Second, the anguish of the fictional character Marina represents a universal real-life experience, the pain of loss and separation from a loved one, which will be with Marina in varying degrees for the rest of her "life", as the actual experience would endure for many people in the real world.

The primary purpose of this volume is to awaken a realization on the part of helping professionals that some people have presenting real-life emotional and psychological distress which cannot be defined or treated as traditional psychopathological problems. Professionals must identify real-life problems — events and reactions to events that are actually being experienced by a person and that must be treated if the person is to live successfully to any degree. This distress, regardless of whether there are psychopathological problems which may complicate identification and treatment, must be differentiated from other forms of psychological and emotional distress. This book also provides professional helpers with a beginning set of guidelines for establishing a course of treatment.

Both the definition of real-life problems and treatment guidelines are based in a recognition that the problems are real — a somewhat obvious but necessary statement which must be made because of our inappropriate tendency to diagnose problems on the basis of criteria applicable to psychopathological disorders, criteria which are not appropriate to helping with real-life problems.

In essence, each of the nine chapters in this volume defines the nature and treatment of real-life problems. The first three chapters provide a foundation for understanding the status of treatment of real-life problems. Chapter 1 defines two categories of real-life problems, temporal real-life problems, which are a part of a person's contemporary experience, and lasting real-life problems, which originate in past experience. Chapter 2 provides an overview of mental health professionals' current attitudes toward real-life problems. Chapter 3 contains a general overview of how existing theoretical approaches can be used in treating real-life problems.

Chapters 4, 5, and 6 are especially significant to understanding the normalcy of people's reactions and experience of real-life problems, as opposed to what the mental health field traditionally has defined as normal. Chapter 4 discusses what normal really means in general terms, and Chapters 5 and 6 apply that general concept to what is normal under the circumstances in temporal (Chapter 5) and lasting (Chapter 6) real-life problems.

Chapters 7 and 8 provide the professional helper with general guidelines for undertaking treatment of real-life problems. Chapter 7 provides general guidelines for treatment. Chapter 8 summarizes and expands discussions throughout the book of the pitfalls professionals must be sensitive to and avoid in order to provide effective support. Finally, Chapter 9 is a brief discussion of research and professional development needs.

Few professionals have acknowledged that the nature of real-life problems differs from and is not dependent upon other forms of psychological and emotional distress. This presents something of a challenge, because specific research on those differences and the appropriate ways for treating many real-life problems is virtually nonexistent. It is possible to gather anecdotal examples and sequelae and to cite research that appears to be related, but the only research that might be applicable is in other areas of diagnosis and treatment. For professionals to recognize that existing research in other areas is applicable requires, first, that one accept or be open to considering that real-life problems do exist outside of psychopathological conditions and, second, that the treatments that are offered must be designed to resolve practical problems related to every day coping needs.

What professional helpers must keep in mind when reading this book is simple. Real-life problems are not and cannot be evaluated as though they originate in some sort of abnormal reaction to an event, nor can they be treated by relying on the theories and methods we traditionally use in the treatment of mental disorders. The key word is "real" — the problems are real, the reactions of those experiencing them are real, and the support and methods for dealing with these problems that professionals offer to people must be based in reality. Theory alone will not suffice.

ACKNOWLEDGEMENTS

I must acknowledge the support of John O. Schwenn, PhD, Chairperson of the Division of Psychology and Special Education, Emporia State University. I must thank Dee Ann Holmes, MS, Coordinator of Observation/Teaching Models, Emporia State University. A special acknowledgment is owed to Gerald B. Fuller, PhD, President, Clinical Psychology Publishing Company, for his patience with this project. Brenda K. Bryant deserves recognition for her exceptional editing of this book.

Cooper B. Holmes
Emporia, Kansas
June 1, 1994

1 REAL-LIFE PROBLEMS: LIKE A LASTING STORM

Defining a real-life problem does not require a detailed list of criteria. The definition is as obvious as it sounds: a problem that has arisen from an actual event in life. However, while the general nature of real-life problems may be evident, a number of related questions must be addressed. Why has the term "real-life" been chosen to describe this class of problems? What is the relationship between real-life problems and mental disorders? What are common types of real-life problems and how are they generated? Do all real-life situations generate real-life problems, and, complementary to that, how do some people escape relatively unscathed from real-life events? Why might people experiencing real-life problems need mental health intervention? What is the frequency of real-life problems? And, finally, what research exists that is related to real-life problems?

WHAT IS MEANT BY "REAL-LIFE" PROBLEM?

For the purpose of this volume, real-life problems do not include short-term and sometimes stressful experiences of everyday life which are experienced by everyone. Rather, a real-life problem refers to significant, enduring psychological and emotional reactions to an actual external event or series of events. The source of these reactions is not a disturbance of psychological functioning. Rather, the person is reacting to an actual event in life. It is understood that any suffering is real for the person experiencing it, whether or not the person is experiencing a psychopathological disorder. The term real-life, then, refers to the source of that anguish.

Psychopathological disorders incorporate emotional and psychological reactions which are not necessarily based in reality, even though a real event may trigger or exacerbate a person's distress when he or she experiences a psychopathological disorder. Considering the fact that the suffering associated with psychopathological disorders is certainly real to the people who experience them, using the term real-life to apply to the category of problems to which this book is dedicated may not be completely satisfactory. However, it is the most accurate term for describing the problems being discussed. An extensive search of literature on psychology, philosophy, sociology, and a wide range of other literature (including mythology) in English and in other languages revealed no other term that might more accurately capture the meaning of real-life problems. The problems are real. The reactions are real. The impact on a person's life is real.

Moreover, one could apply the phrase "lasting storm" to ongoing mental disorders, as well as to real-life problems. A person who is chronically depressed or anxious or who suffers frightening loss of contact with reality could certainly be considered to be in a lasting storm. His or her pain and suffering are no less real than that of a person suffering a real-life problem. However, the source of pain for a person experiencing a mental disorder rests in a disturbance of psychological processes such as poor self-esteem, unresolved emotional conflicts, or unfounded beliefs. It would be appropriate to describe such disturbances using terms like psychopathological, abnormality, mental disorder, and mental illness. To clearly identify instances where a person's reactions and behavior result from a disturbance of psychological functioning, the term psychopathological will be used throughout this book.

THE RELATION BETWEEN PSYCHOPATHOLOGICAL AND REAL-LIFE PROBLEMS

Psychopathological and real-life problems are not mutually exclusive. There is certainly no reason to assume that a person with a psychopathological disorder could not have a real-life problem as well. In fact, it would be surprising if a significant number of these individuals did not experience both psychological and real-life problems. The fact that both types of problems might exist at the same time requires that helpers demonstrate sensitivity, wisdom, and skill to tease out real-life aspects from the psychopathological aspects of the person's behaviors and address them accordingly. Saying that this effort might be quite difficult would be making a gross understatement.

Are all real-life problems psychopathological? Clearly, they are not. In the sense that reacting to real-life events involves sometimes very strong, if not overwhelming, emotions and life changes, the reactions a person might have are clearly psychological. However, they are not necessarily psychopathological, because the source of the reaction is not a disturbance of normal psychological functions. Referring to the consequences of suicide to the survivors, Rynearson (1981) noted, "Uncertainty, anxiety, hopelessness and despair are not necessarily pathologic of unresolved, unconscious conflict because they consistently accompany such an enormous existential trauma" (p. 85). It is quite possible for a person with a real-life problem to continue functioning in a productive, effective manner in spite of the strain of the lasting storm (e.g., see Norton, 1989, and Wholey, 1992).

Although this discussion may appear to be a somewhat academic exercise, there is a practical purpose: To establish the need for different approaches to helping people with real-life problems. If a person is suffering due to a disturbance of psychological functioning, it is evident that helping the person involves establishing or reestablishing normal psychological functioning through whatever means is necessary (resolving a conflict, working through irrational beliefs, building confidence or self esteem, medication, and so on). Once the client has re-established normal psychological functioning, the problem is resolved or, if you will, "cured." Because the cause is psychopathological, the cure rests in removing the pathology.

However, if the person's responses are due to some real-life event, the reactions of the person must be understood and dealt with in a fundamentally different way. The problem cannot be resolved by techniques that are geared toward the removal of psychopathological causes. There is no underlying pathology to be removed. Realizing this basic fact is an absolute necessity if one is to help a person with a real-life problem and to avoid the mistakes that will be noted later in this book.

TYPES OF REAL-LIFE PROBLEMS

The circumstances that create real-life problems fall into two general groups, which form the foundation for the definition of two categories of real-life problems, temporal real-life problems and lasting real-life problems. Understanding the two categories depends upon an understanding of the effect of time and the possibility of change.

On the day a person comes to the professional for help, the real-life problems he or she brings will naturally relate to current or past experience. Of course, many actual events and people's reactions to them fall into the normal, expected category. Such events create transient stress for a person, but those stresses are relatively mild, quite resolvable for a person with normal psychological resources, and may lead to personal growth. For example, graduating from college, marrying, having a child, and retiring present some degrees of stress as a person adjusts to related changes. These types of adjustments do not reach the level of severity that is associated with what is referred to here as a real-life problem. Real-life problems are life-altering events that do not necessarily offer a positive outcome for the person.

Temporal Real-Life Problems

Temporal real-life problems are not the daily annoyances and challenges we all experience, however great they may appear to be at the time. Rather, the problem arises from significant, life-altering events that are still being experienced. In the sense that temporal implies occurring now, the event causing the problem is occurring in today's world, and the person is reacting to an existing situation. The problem may come to a conclusion in the future, but the hope that future events may alleviate the situation provides little relief for the person in distress.

To effectively address a temporal real-life problem, the person experiencing the problem and those who are trying to help must deal with the reality of what the person is experiencing. Neither the person nor the helper should approach efforts to resolve distress as if the origin of the problem were psychopathological. It is not. Moreover, life situations outside the person's control may change, the person may learn new ways to cope, or the person may learn ways to change the situation itself. Thus, the possibility of change offers hope of eventual resolution of the problem. Nonetheless, the distress must be endured, and the person's efforts to cope with that distress require support.

Examples of temporal real-life problems are: having to stand by and watch as an adolescent child practices prostitution to support a drug habit and risks getting AIDS; coping with a loved one being convicted of a crime and having to serve a long prison term; being cut off from contact with a parent or child who has joined a cult; living in a family suffering the effects of abject poverty; being homeless; being falsely accused of sexual abuse; coping with the everyday demands of living with a person experiencing chronic serious mental illness. Each of these events is contemporary, ongoing, and may come to an end (with or without the person's intervention). Each event is also life-altering, although there are aspects of each which may still offer an opportunity for change.

Lasting Real-Life Problems

Lasting real-life problems stem from a completed event or series of events. A day or a decade may have passed since the event occurred, and the opportunity to change what occurred has passed. Also, the experience was of such proportions that it permanently altered the person's life. A person's experience of a lasting real-life problem forms an underpinning for that person's reactions to many, if not all life experiences following the event that created the problem. The experience may not overwhelm all aspects of the person's remaining life, but it may color even what for most of us might be insignificant events and subtlety alter emotional and psychological responses. The most common description one hears of such an event's impact is that the person's life "has never been the same since."

One must keep in mind when considering lasting real-life problems that the psychological and emotional damage of the event has been done; there is no possibility of resolution through any action that might be taken by the person or the helper. However, to say that resolution is not possible is not the same as saying that there is nothing one can do to help the person deal with conflict and distress. (See following chapters.)

Although some temporal real-life problems can be resolved and a person's emotional and psychological well-being restored, the fact that an event ends does not necessarily mean that the distress associated with it has been resolved. What is initially a temporal problem can become a lasting real-life problem. For example, a soldier taken prisoner by the enemy will have certain temporal real-life problems to face — finding proper nourishment, dealing with health issues, losing friends to violence and disease, suffering physical punishment, and so forth. Once the soldier is freed from imprisonment and physical health is restored, he or she is likely to endure lasting psychological effects as well. Some individuals have experiences that are so personally traumatic that the effects of those experiences endure throughout the remainder of their lives. How can one forever resolve the distress of beating one's child to death in a fit of rage, or witnessing the horrible injury of a loved one in an accident, or enduring the psychological and emotional distress of a vicious physical attack by a mugger?

Such events may lead to reactions that clearly fit into the posttraumatic stress disorder category (American Psychiatric Association, 1987). However, other equally devastating situations are not as easily classified. How does one fully classify such events as destroying one's relationship with a child or a cherished friend by making a thoughtless statement in a moment of anger, destroying a marriage by having an affair, having to give up a child for adoption, being separated from a grandchild when one's son or daughter surrenders the grandchild for adoption, or experiencing the regret of being unable to heal the pain one has caused by turning one's back on the suffering of a friend?

In some cases, a component of the distress experienced in lasting real-life problems may meet the criteria for being a form of mental disorder, and complete treatment of both the real-life problem and the mental disorder must be provided. Indeed, certain mental disorders require that an identifiable stressor — a real-life experience — precipitate a person's reaction, posttraumatic stress disorder and adjustment disorder being two examples. However, lasting real-life problems are not necessarily associated with mental disorder, although any person, even one experiencing a real-life problem, also may be experiencing some form of mental disorder. A person's reaction to a real-life problem may be influenced by such a disorder, but the disorder itself is not the problem, nor will treatment of the disorder alone resolve the person's concerns about and reactions to the real-life problem she or he may be experiencing.

Acknowledging the possibility of resolution is a key to understanding the difference between temporal and lasting real-life problems. Temporal problems at least allow some hope that the problem may attenuate in the future. However, there has been no empirical investigation on the lasting effects of situations that are seemingly resolved, and it cannot be said with certainty whether there are lasting effects even if the situation is eventually attenuated.

At the same time, it is clearly possible that after a situation has been resolved, there may be effects that will never be totally overcome. The more traumatic an experience may be, the more likely it is that effects may be long-term or permanent. For example, for survivors of the Holocaust, who have been extensively studied, lasting effects have been the norm rather than the exception (e.g., Baider, Peretz, & DeNour, 1992; Eaton, Signal, & Weinfield, 1982).

At a lesser level of stressor, it is uncertain whether everything could be considered as resolved once a situation is over. For example, in a relationship where one person is emotionally drained for years by the actions of another person, is it possible for the relationship between those two people to ever be "normal" again? Could a teacher falsely accused of child sexual abuse ever feel completely free with children again, even after his or her innocence had been established?

Summary

Thus, in considering the differences between temporal and lasting real-life problems, the following questions are key: Is the source of the problem still acting on the problem? Is there possibility for resolution? Even in instances where a person has no control over specific events, to what degree can he or she take steps to ameliorate the effects of the event? If the answer to these questions is, "The event is still taking place, and there is a possibility that it will be resolved or for the person to influence the outcome," then the problem is probably a temporal real-life problem. If the answer is, "What's done is done; change and resolution is no longer possible, and the person must learn to live with the outcome," then the problem is a lasting real-life problem.

DO HIGHLY STRESSFUL EVENTS ALWAYS PRODUCE REAL-LIFE PROBLEMS?

It is reasonable to ask if overwhelming events always produce real-life problems. The answer is a very certain, "No." Some people are graced with psychological strength and a philosophy about life that allow them to undergo immensely difficult situations with coping abilities that anyone would envy. Each of us has known people like that. In fact, some researchers have studied which factors may account for differences in coping styles (e.g., Cohen & Wills, 1985; Foy, Resnick, Sipprelle, & Carol, 1987; Kobasa, Maddi, & Kahn, 1982). Unfortunately, the research is not conclusive about this issue. Essentially, we do not know why some people cope so well with a stressful event and others do not. The personal qualities and other factors which apparently contribute to a person's ability to cope are diverse. For some people, the coping tool may be deep religious conviction, while for others it may be a remarkably tolerant attitude about life that comes from some source we do not understand. If we knew how they managed to acquire these abilities, or what was unique about the individuals themselves, we might be better able to help other people acquire similar abilities.

All we now know is that some people have a remarkable ability to deal with overwhelming situations and keep going. Given that some people manage to escape serious psychological consequences from a real-life event, it is unavoidable that one would ask if people who are permanently affected are in some way abnormal. Did they have existing problems with their psychological strength or stability before events occurred? As noted previously, it is certainly possible that a person could have both a real-life problem and a psy-

chopathological problem, but the presence of a real-life problem does not
necessarily indicate some kind of psychopathology. It must be recognized
that these people are dealing with real-life events of very significant proportions. The fact that they do not escape emotional sequelae, as a few supreme-
ly well-adjusted people might do, does not mean they are abnormal. To make
such a comparison would be like comparing a self-actualizing person to the
more typical person. The fact that most people do not have the resources of a
self-actualizing person does not make the average person abnormal or psychologically deficient. The fact that some people endure life-long sequelae to
real-life events without becoming overwhelmed simply indicates that some
situations are more traumatic than we could reasonably expect any average
person to endure with no consequences. The problem is the situation, not the
person.

THE NEED FOR MENTAL HEALTH INTERVENTION

If it is correct that most people with real-life problems suffer no psychopathology, it is reasonable to ask why there is a need for mental health
intervention. The answer is that these people function within the normal
range, but that is not the same as functioning at their optimal level and being
as free of emotional concerns as they could be. It is quite possible that their
lives could be enhanced in some way. Seeking enhancement does not mean
there are serious problems; rather, it is recognition that there is potential for
positive change in some aspect of the person's life. Thus, counseling related
to real-life problems is analogous to marriage or job enhancement counseling.

FREQUENCY OF REAL-LIFE PROBLEMS

At this point, it is not possible to state how many people have real-life
problems. If the head count included all people undergoing actual events, the
frequency would be 100%. All people will face points of adjustment in their
lives that are based in real-life events, but, as previously noted, real-life problems do not include everyday types of adjustments all people make many
times throughout their lives. However, even limiting such a survey to the
more serious level of real-life events, it would still not be possible to develop
a reasonable estimate of rate of occurrence. Psychological literature addresses
real-life problems that have a psychopathological component to them (e.g.,
posttraumatic stress disorder, adjustment disorders), as well as sources of distress (e.g., grieving and family conflict). However, the literature does not pro-

vide much information on people who are suffering real-life problems without psychopathological features and, especially, on those who quietly suffer and never seek any type of professional assistance. Common sense, and a cursory exposure to the media, however, clearly indicates that real-life problems are far from rare. It would seem that in some ways an attempt to verify the number and nature of real-life problems is an attempt to verify the obvious. There are many people who are enduring real-life problems.

REAL-LIFE PROBLEMS AND CURRENT LITERATURE

In spite of the lack of direct research, the mental health field is not completely devoid of information on the topic of dealing with real-life problems. For example, Figley and McCubbin (1983), McCubbin and Figley (1983), Norton (1989), and Everstine and Everstine (1993) have written books that address various real-life problems, and there are numerous articles on specific real-life events and related effects. To name only a few, Dreman (1989) has written about the problems experienced by children of victims of terrorism, Finkelstein (1988) about the impact of the death of a parent, Cohen and Roth (1987) about the aftereffects of rape, Martin and Elmer (1992) on surviving being a battered child, Charmaz (1991) on the experience of physical illnesses, and Ness and Pfeffer (1990) and Rynearson (1981) on the effects of a suicide on survivors. However, the literature is scattered over a wide number of different content areas. Moreover, coverage tends to be uneven (i.e., some topics receive rather extensive coverage, while others are virtually ignored).

There are specific areas of the health and mental health fields that routinely deal with real-life problems whose source is clearly not psychological, for example, rehabilitation counseling, grief counseling, neuropsychology, and medical psychology. In each of these areas, the practitioner must help the client come to grips with some serious, potentially life-altering situation. Although the emotional reactions are psychological, the root cause is not. In addition, there are therapists in the mental health field who work with real-life situations that also include a degree of psychopathological involvement, for example, posttraumatic stress disorders (e.g., Davidson & Foa, 1992). The literature on some of these topics is extensive. Unfortunately, the literature on other types of real-life problems, such as grandparents losing a grandchild or parents coping with the imprisonment of a child, is not nearly so great.

Even with the extensive (albeit selective) literature in some areas, the fact remains that it would be a Herculean effort for any one person to become familiar with all of it. Fortunately, when one looks across the literature from

different specialties and for different problems, it is possible to identify a fair-
ly common set of guidelines for dealing with real-life problems. The ideas
and concepts are not a perfect fit, as might be expected when one draws from
areas as diverse as psychotherapy, rehabilitation counseling, Holocaust sur-
vivor counseling, and counseling families coping with a family member who
is experiencing serious mental disturbance. However, it is certainly worth-
while to bring these ideas together, as will be done in the remainder of this
volume.

2 THE MENTAL HEALTH FIELD AND REAL-LIFE PROBLEMS

The purpose of this chapter is to take a close, objective look at how well the mental health field is meeting the needs of individuals with real-life problems. This is not an easy task, given that little literature is available that specifically addresses the issue. There is some direct information, of course, and some material that can be extrapolated to apply to real-life problems.

As was noted in the previous chapter, within the mental health field there are certain specializations that routinely address real-life problems. For example, rehabilitation workers help people incorporate a loss of physical or mental function and go on living. Grief counselors help people survive the emotional trauma associated with the loss of a loved one. Medical psychologists help people learn to control intractable pain and to live in spite of it. Neuropsychologists help clients and families cope with the lasting effects of head injuries and illnesses. Social workers support people coping with homelessness and unemployment. Therapists of many professions help combatants and noncombatants traumatized by war.

This list of specialized workers does not exhaust the list of mental health professionals who are trained to work with real-life problems, but it does point out that professionals choosing to work with real-life problems must have specialized training in order to be able to be effective. The goal of this book is not to address the training needs of those who already have specialized training. Rather, it is to address the nature and content of additional training needed by mental health workers whose primary responsibility is the diagnosis and treatment of psychological disorders. In other words, how can we enhance the effectiveness of therapists found in mental health centers, psychiatric hospitals, and general private practice who are confronted by the need to treat people with real-life problems?

As already noted, most people with real-life problems will not have psychopathological disorders. However, their treatment is typically provided by professionals who are not usually trained in working with normal, productive individuals and, therefore, are not trained to work with many of the people who are experiencing the kinds of problems described in this book. Given this current lack of training, it is reasonable to ask whether diagnosticians and therapists who work in general mental health settings should be able to offer help to people with real-life problems, especially if the people do not suffer psychopathological sequelae. To answer this question, we must acknowledge that professionals in the mental health field already provide services to people with real-life problems who are not suffering psychopathological problems. Thus, the answer to the question is definitely, "Yes, mental health professionals need appropriate training."

The DSM-III-R V code category (American Psychiatric Association, 1987) is in part designated to address the needs of people seeking psychiatric help who do not have a diagnosable psychological disorder, but who are experiencing distress associated with ordinary life events (e.g., academic problem, marital problem, uncomplicated bereavement). Mental health workers routinely present workshops on topics such as divorce, parenting, study skills, marriage enrichment, personal growth and fulfillment, and vocational enhancement. Of course, these examples of sought-for help do not involve the severe situations that characterize a real-life problem, but the point is that mental health workers clearly address many issues that do not involve psychopathology.

People undergoing the lasting storms of life are in emotional pain and should be able to seek and receive dependable help from the mental health field. After all, who is better qualified than a mental health worker to understand and help with emotional concerns? Given the fact that people already seek out such support, how does the mental health field fare on this count? Unfortunately, information on effectiveness of mental health treatment in this area is limited, and in most cases reported data are not directly related to the issue. To this author's knowledge, there are no data on how many people with real-life problems seek counseling but do not pursue it because they cannot find related counseling or found supposedly appropriate counseling that was offered not to be helpful. However, there are data from three related research areas that offer useful information about success or failure in helping with real-life problems: studies on psychotherapy dropouts, studies on dissatisfaction with mental health services, and articles on reasons for the rise in the number of self-help groups. The evidence that is available strongly suggests that the field is not living up to its potential to help these people.

PSYCHOTHERAPY DROPOUTS

A number of studies have addressed the rate of and reasons for clients discontinuing or, as it is commonly called, dropping out of psychotherapy. Baekeland and Lundwall (1975), in a review of the literature, found that from 20% to 57% of general psychiatric patients do not return after the first visit and that 31% to 56% attended no more than four sessions. From 33% to 50% of group therapy patients drop out and from 32% to 79% of psychiatric inpatients on open wards sign out against medical advice. Pekarik (1983) found that of 64 clients, 41 (64.1%) dropped out of therapy prematurely. Pekarik cited other studies noting that about 40% of mental health center clients attended only one or two sessions and that 20% of private practice clients dropped out within two visits. In a later article, Pekarik (1985) reviewed the literature on psychotherapy dropouts and offered suggestions about dealing with them.

After studying psychotherapy dropouts, Stahler and Eisenman (1987) suggested that perhaps dropouts leave treatment because they are basically stronger to begin with and need only a few sessions to help them address the presenting problems. Stahler and Eisenman offered some data to support their conclusion. However, based on clinical experiences and the comments shared by clients, students, and colleagues, this author cannot avoid considering the possibility that, in fact, some of the dropouts were people who sought help and simply found none.

DISSATISFACTION WITH MENTAL HEALTH SERVICES

Studies on dissatisfaction with mental health services have usually focused on families with a severely psychologically disturbed member (a real-life problem) and the family's reaction to those services. Hatfield (1978) found that nearly half of the respondents, who were from families of clients experiencing schizophrenia, reported that mental health services were of no value to them. In a discussion of her work and the work of others, Bernheim (1989) noted several reasons why family members are dissatisfied with mental health professionals: "In sum, many families object strenuously to being treated as the 'unidentified patient.' They find this notion counterintuitive, insulting, and not conducive to fruitful help" (1989, p. 562). Also addressing the stresses of living with a severely mentally ill family member, Holden and Lewine (1982) found that 74% of their respondents (again, from families of clients experiencing schizophrenia) were dissatisfied with mental health professionals who were treating their family members. Holden and Lewine noted that mental health professionals focus on the family's role in the development and maintenance of the problems, with a concomitant de-emphasis on the impact of the problem on the family. The families described the mental health professionals as vague and evasive, providing little useful information about the client's problem, treatment, and prognosis, and as basically ignoring the needs of the family as a whole. Holden and Lewine noted, "Many families reported that their involvement with professionals left them feeling guilty and defensive" (1982, p. 627). The authors also noted, "Generally, the respondents had a *realistic* [emphasis added] picture of the illness and its prognosis. Repeatedly, families reported a need for *realistic and practical guidance* [emphasis added]" (p. 632). Rappaport et al. (1985) discussed some of the attitudes expressed by mental health workers that interfere with helping chronically mentally ill persons, for example, an unwillingness to work with the client outside the professional office and an unwillingness to get involved in the client's everyday life and concerns.

Referring to mental health services in general, Murstein and Fontaine (1993) surveyed a random sample of individuals. They found that 24.07% of the people who had been in therapy rated it as being of modest help (9 of 54 people), no help (3 of 54), or actually worsening the situation (1 of 54). Nineteen percent of these people would not suggest that someone else consult a mental health person. Less recent studies (e.g., Holden & Lewine, 1982) reported similar findings about dissatisfaction. Realizing that dissatisfaction is a matter of personal perspective, it is still the case that one-fourth of the people treated did not find mental health services to be of any significant value. If this result seems unduly pessimistic, consider the statements drawn from the American Psychological Association Science Directorate's Science 1993 Weekend, which was entitled "Contributions of Basic Research to Applied Problems: Does Behavior Change Permanently?", as reported on by Adler (1993). Adler noted, "Mental health experts often have little success in permanently curing clients of their ills..." (p. 17) and "Despite a wealth of approaches and techniques, therapists often are unable to make their clients permanently feel or function normally, psychologists said at the symposium" (p. 17). Finally, Adler noted "therapists aren't really helping that many folks to a clinically significant degree, said Neil Jackson, Ph.D., a psychologist at the University of Washington" (p. 17).

Based on these and similar reports, the inevitable conclusion is that the mental health field is falling short of its potential to help many people experiencing clinically based distress, and there is no reason to assume the situation is any different for people suffering real-life problems. In fact, it is reasonable to assume that people with real-life problems are being even less well-served than individuals with psychopathological problems, as the next section will show.

RISE IN THE NUMBER OF SELF-HELP GROUPS

In articles dealing with the increase in the number of self-help groups, virtually all authors have either explicitly stated or strongly implied that self-help groups have grown in number and diversity because the participants are not receiving the help they need through the usual psychological channels (e.g., Holden & Lewine, 1982; Jacobs & Goodman, 1989; Lieberman, 1986; Rappaport et al., 1985; Tyler, 1980). Tyler (1980) stated, "For the support and understanding they need in struggling with their problems, many individuals are turning to self-help groups rather than psychotherapists. By the year 2,000, this will have become standard practice" (p. 20). Holden and Lewine (1989) echoed the same point when they stated, "Such self-help groups often form when members' needs are not met through more traditional channels" (p. 626). All of the studies leave little doubt about why the number of self-help groups is growing: The mental health field is not providing what a large number of people feel they need. Jacobs and Goodman (1989) put the number of self-help group participants at nearly 7 million. Recognizing that some people may be using both modes of help, this is still a significant number of people to be seeking help other than that available through mental health channels.

WHAT THESE RELATED STUDIES TELL US

Reports on psychotherapy dropouts, dissatisfaction with mental health services, and the proliferation of self-help groups point to unfortunate deficiencies in the mental health system's ability to provide useful services to a large number of potential clients, many of whom, it is reasonably certain, suffer from some type of real-life problem. Why this is so is a matter more of speculation than of empirical fact; however, as already noted, there are four plausible reasons for mental health professionals' failure to provide effective service to people with real-life problems: lack of experience with normal individuals; a tendency to view clients and their concerns as expressions of psychopathological problems rather than as real-life, rational concerns; lack of training and experience in working with many of the real-life problems, which generates an understandable avoidance of working with these clients; and a tendency to avoid working with problems that have no real cure. The rest of this chapter will explore these four points in greater detail.

Relative Lack of Experience Working With Normal People

All mental health workers have friends, families, and colleagues, and other acquaintances who are normal. However, the focus of their interests and training is on the diagnosis and treatment of abnormality, and their lack of training and experience in treating people who have no definable psy-chopathology — normal people — is problematic. Consider how few under-graduate and graduate courses in normal psychology are required in order for a person to obtain a degree of any kind. One must also consider that mental health workers have daily contact with clients who have psychopathological disorders and only occasional contact with individuals who do not. After a while, it is probable that every person will be perceived as having some kind of mental problem. Looking for, expecting, and dealing with mental disorders becomes the norm. This perception exacerbates the inability of professionals to evaluate and treat the normal person presenting a real-life problem. In an often cited quotation, Henry Murray (1951) stated, "Were an analyst to be confronted by that much-heralded but still missing specimen of the human race—the normal man—he would be struck dumb, for once, through lack of appropriate ideas" (p. 436). Murray is not the only well-known individual to express this sentiment. In 1962, Grinker, Grinker, and Timberlake presented the results of a study of psychologically healthy college males. In that article, Roy Grinker, Sr., described his reaction to assessing these mentally healthy young men by writing, "The impact of these interviews on me was startling! Here was a type of young man I had not met before in my role as a psychia-trist and rarely in my personal life" (p. 405). The eminence of these authors gives us reason to pause and consider their message—mental health workers are not as comfortable and familiar as they should be with persons who suffer no psychopathological problems. This undoubtedly contributes to the issue discussed in the next section.

The Tendency Toward Making Psychological Interpretations— Psychologizing

Because of their interest in psychopathological processes, mental health workers tend to see psychological disturbance when it is not really present in the client, that is, they "psychologize." There is ample support for this conclusion. One need look no further than the present controversy over repressed memories to see how easy it to psychologize a problem. Certainly, Loftus has been a voice of reason in this matter (Loftus, 1993), pointing out some of the highly questionable tactics and findings (also see Denton, 1993, and Tavris, 1993). Simply stated, in some and many more than a few cases, therapists are diagnosing problems that are not really there. My own work (Holmes, 1992) on the misdiagnosis of neurological conditions as psychiatric disorders clearly reveals the tendency to diagnosis psychological disorders because they are expected, even in cases of clear organic involvement. Although it has been justifiably criticized on a number of counts, the famous article by Rosenhan (1973) on pseudopatients did show how therapists may construe normal behavior (e.g., taking notes) as a sign of mental disorder.

Virtually any source on crosscultural counseling will present examples of how a specific action or lack of action may be misinterpreted by those not familiar with a client's culture (Everett, Proctor, & Cartmell, 1989; Sue & Sue, 1992; Westermeyer, 1987). For example, Everett, Proctor, and Cartmell (1987) pointed out that some Native American individuals avoid eye contact to show respect, yet this may be misinterpreted by some mental health service providers as a sign of avoidance or other possible psychological problems which must be investigated. Gong-Guy, Cravens, and Patterson (1991) wrote the following about mental health services to refugees:

> Mental health practitioners attach relatively greater significance to psychological issues than do refugees. Refugees cite as their most pressing problems lack of English skills, family separation, unemployment, limited funds, lack of transportation, and insufficient child care. Depression, anxiety and other psychological problems are either absent or mentioned less frequently (Moon & Tashima, 1982). Practitioners who focus on addressing emotional issues to the point of excluding pragmatic issues are perceived as unresponsive to the needs of the refugee, and are unlikely to be seen as a relevant resource. (p. 644)

In regard to downplaying real-life concerns while focusing on psychological issues, McCarthy, Reese, Schueneman, and Reese (1991) commented on mental health services for working class women. They stated:

> When counsellors move too far beyond immediate concerns, such as where the client will sleep that night and how she will feed her children this month, and attempt instead to focus on "self-growth," "improving the client's social status," or some other meta-goal, the client may feel as if she has failed in counselling.... What often happens in such cases is that the client terminates, and that may actually be her healthiest response. (p. 589)

The authors went on to note the importance of setting realistic and concrete counseling goals.

In one study, Langer and Abelson (1974) presented a videotaped interview of a young man to two groups of clinicians (totalling 40 individuals), and both groups were asked to rate the adjustment of the young man. One group was told that the young man was a job applicant. The other group was told that the young man was a psychiatric patient. The clinicians who were told the young man was a psychiatric patient rated the man's adjustment lower than did the clinicians who told he was a job applicant. Langer and Abelson noted, "Once an individual enters a therapist's office for consultation, he has labeled himself 'patient.' From the very start of the session, the orientation of the conversation may be quite negative" (p. 9). By negative, the authors meant there was a focus on negative rather than adaptive aspects of the client's behavior and personality. Rynearson (1981), referring to the effects of suicide on survivors, stated, "One of the classic errors in clinical research is to view the subject as inherently pathologic rather than adaptive, to reductively anticipate disorder rather than equilibration" (p. 84).

Both Kaminer (1992) and Tavris (1992) criticized therapists (especially "pop" therapists) for taking normal, everyday behaviors and feelings and turning them into diagnosable (therefore, treatable) disorders. Both authors pointed out the popularity of certain "problems" and the vagueness of criteria by which they are judged.

After acknowledging his being perplexed by normal people, Murray (1951) went on to note, "I am suffering one of the commonest ailments of our age—trained disability" (p. 436). He was referring to the tendency of mental health workers to couch almost any word or action in terms of some deeper psychological process. Davison and Neale (1994) perhaps summed up this point when they stated:

> The attribution literature makes the basic assumption that people care what the causes of their behavior are. This central idea is the brainchild of psychologists whose business it is to explain behavior. It may be that psychologists have projected their own need to explain behavior on to other people! Lay-people may simply not reflect on why they act and feel as they do to the same extent that psychologists do. (p. 238)

The tendency to erroneously view behavior, thoughts, and emotions as manifestations of psychological disturbance leads clients to feel, with justification, that their concerns are being misunderstood. Over my years of clinical work I have found a consistent sense of resentment on the part of clients when they feel their concerns are being turned into something they are not. The tendency on the part of a mental health worker to view justifiable guilt, sadness, or worry as a manifestation of psychopathological processes can only serve to distance the client from the worker. Further, to consider a client as being unwilling to let go of a concern because of some psychological need to keep it completely ignores the possibility that the client would gladly let go of it if he or she could, but the problem will not let go of the client. Under these circumstances, McCarthy, Reese, Schueneman, and Reese (1991) noted the best thing a client could do would be to terminate therapy.

Lack of Experience with Real-Life Problems

A lack of experience with real-life problems is obviously an impediment to helping. Two factors contribute to this inexperience. First, there are few academic courses designed to provide mental health professionals with basic skills in addressing real-life problems. Second, it is highly likely that people with real-life problems are not deeply involved with the mental health system. Thus, the typical mental health worker does not have the opportunity to accrue knowledge of a large number of cases from which he or she could build knowledge, confidence, and techniques. Given the large number of events that would qualify as creating real-life problems, acquiring experience is a daunting, but not insurmountable task. Workshops, reading, case discussions among colleagues, and other professional interactions may provide at least a general background for addressing these problems.

The Need for Therapeutic Success

Simply stated, the goal of a helping professional is to assist the client in resolving whatever brought him or her into the sessions. Every person needs to feel his or her work is productive and meaningful. In the mental health field, feeling productive and valued depends upon having a belief that one is helping people achieve closure to their concerns, often through the process of resolving psychopathological issues. If one's work never or rarely helps clients achieve closure and clients' problems are not resolvable in the usual sense of the word, the mental health worker is likely to become frustrated and may question the value of his or her work. Even worse, the helping professional may begin to question the client's motivation to get better. Mental health workers are no different than anyone else: They need to feel rewarded in their work.

Unfortunately, one need look only as far as certain areas of the mental health practice to see the avoidance of some types of clients because working with them is perceived as minimally rewarding. As a practicing psychologist and a professor who has helped train many psychologists, to no one's great amazement, this author can state that working with chronically mentally ill clients is considered by most therapists and soon-to-be therapists as unrewarding and unproductive. Most mental health workers avoid assuming such roles. (See Rappaport et al., 1985, for a discussion of some of the attitudes and practices of mental health workers that interfere with working with chronic patients.) Work with substance abuse clients and criminals is also perceived as being professionally unrewarding and is avoided by many therapists. In other words, therapists see work with clients whose treatment offers a reasonable chance of success in a reasonable amount of time as being more rewarding, exciting, interesting, and productive.

Real-life problems clearly fit into the category that most mental health workers would like to avoid, given the usual definition of successful therapy. Lacking true resolution, lasting real-life problems have no end, and temporal real-life problems have only indefinite, unpredictable points of closure, if closure is possible at all. In those cases where the immediate real-life problem may be partially relieved (e.g., a rebellious child settles down), all the previous months or, more likely, years of turmoil will have left their mark. Both lasting and temporal real-life problems often have no point of final resolution. The therapists will not be able to achieve the sense of closure and fulfillment found when a task is completed. Therapeutic work with real-life problems is very likely to be long-term and ongoing. It is not surprising that therapists might avoid taking on such cases. The apparent solution is for mental health workers to redefine success as do professionals who work in areas such as rehabilitation, treatment of chronic patients, and pain management (e.g., Phillips, 1988). Success in these cases is defined as the client making an effective adjustment in spite of the problem.

It is important to conclude this chapter by noting that the purpose of this discussion is not to indict the mental health field for failure to meet the needs of any client or group of clients. Has the mental health field failed completely in addressing real-life concerns? No. However, the meager literature on this topic does strongly indicate that the field must pay more attention to real-life problems.

3 THE ROLE OF THEORIES IN HELPING

There is a confusing array of theories to explain human behavior, both normal and abnormal. Depending on whose categorization one uses, there are 40 or more theories of personality and treatment. The purpose of this chapter is not to present a detailed discussion of these various theories; rather, it is to discuss the influence of theory, any theory, in the process of understanding and helping individuals with real-life problems. The discussion will address common groups of theories, rather than specific theories (e.g., humanistic theories in general, rather than Rogers's theory specifically).

Although this chapter is not meant to be a comprehensive exposition of theories of personality and treatment, some general comments are needed to set the stage for the remainder of the discussion. First, it is important to note that many of the alleged differences across theories are more semantic than real. That is, the theories agree on a concept but disagree on what to call it. All theories recognize that a person cannot be immediately aware of every memory, thought, and emotion, but some theoreticians call this the unconscious, while others simply say the material is out of awareness. There is no serious disagreement over the concept, regardless of what it is called. Of course there are some real differences among the theories, but the differences pale in comparison to the similarities. When teaching, I even tell my students that a good operational definition of understanding the theories is reaching the point where they say to themselves, "I've heard this before."

Second, there is a tendency to confuse theory with fact, especially among new clinicians. It is a fact that people behave in certain ways. It is interpretation (theory) when we try to explain why they do so. Whether or not one's superego is overactive is a matter of theory, not fact. Whether or not there are underlying reasons for behavior is a matter of interpretation, not established truth.

This is a crucial point in considering how to approach real-life problems, because in too many cases theories take on lives of their own to the point that they dictate what clinicians hear and, more importantly, how clients' concerns are conceptualized and treated. Blind allegiance to a particular theory leads into the trap of finding what is expected because the theory says it must be there, and, even worse, it leads to the tendency to ignore what does not fit the theory. This point has been forcefully made by Sulloway (1991) in reference to psychoanalysis, Masson (1988) about a number of theories, and many other health professionals.

The clinician must be alert to the possibility of formulating a client's concerns in some theoretical framework that is, in fact, inappropriate. Kennedy (1981), stating that psychological treatment in America has been democratized (his term), noted, "...it has also given birth to hackneyed and naive models of how to help people with their emotional problems" (p. 21). He also stated, "Sadly enough, just such people, awash in both good will and good intentions, become victims of oversimplified psychological notions and prefabricated counseling structures" (p. 21). Finally, Kennedy noted, "Yet another sign of this is the determined effort on the part of some helpers to apply a model of counseling whether it fits or not" (p. 22). Perhaps George Kelly (1955) summed this up best when he wrote, "If you don't know what's wrong with a client, ask him; he may tell you" (p. 201).

Theory does serve a purpose and may be helpful in dealing with persons with real-life problems. However, real-life problems incorporate a broad spectrum of causes and consequences and occur in people with vastly different personalities. It makes little sense to use the same psychological approach with all clients, whether they are experiencing psychopathological or real-life problems and regardless of a client's specific difficulties. To date, we have accumulated little empirical fact about why people turn out the way they do and why they act in certain ways and not in others. The assumption that the mental health field has developed to the point where one theory from among the many theories presented can explain and treat all difficulties is unwarranted and potentially harmful. Using a single approach with all clients is certain to fail in many cases and to succeed only when the theory by chance happens to be appropriate for addressing the client's problems. The use of a single theory with all clients, regardless of presenting problems, is directly equivalent to a physician prescribing only one medicine regardless of a patient's illness. To think that a responsible physician would do that is absurd, yet many well-meaning mental health workers prescribe the same treatment for all their clients.

Is the use of a single approach common enough in the mental health field to warrant concern? Data indicates that the majority of psychologists providing therapy do use a specific theoretical orientation. Smith (1982) surveyed psychologists and found that 41.20% reported using an eclectic approach and 58.80% using a specific theoretical approach. The three categories of approaches reported as more frequently used were psychoanalytic (10.84%), cognitive-behavioral (10.36%), and "other" (9.16%). Of course, data did not reveal how strictly the clinicians adhered to their reported theories, but the survey did demonstrate that the majority of therapists endorsed a single approach.

In evaluating the effectiveness of using a single-theory approach to treat real-life problems, two major points must be emphasized. First, because many people with real-life problems will not have an underlying psychopathological disorder, trying to understand and treat them in terms of most theories is problematical. Some type of explanation of normal behavior is incorporated in most theories, but the primary emphasis of theories is on psychopathology. (See the section in Chapter 2 on lack of experience with normal people.) Trying to mold a person's real-life problem into a limited theoretical framework presents two very real possibilities for failure. First, because the theory influences what is asked and discussed, the problem may not be seen accurately. Second, naturally the theory will influence how the problem is conceptualized and, in the end, how it is treated; if the theory is inappropriate, the treatment likely will be inappropriate.

The second major point is that most theories and associated treatments are aimed at achieving resolution of the client's problem. As noted previously, resolution is simply not possible in many cases of lasting real-life problems and is difficult and ill-defined in many cases of temporal real-life problems. Using a theoretical approach designed primarily to achieve some kind of closure is obviously ill-suited to the task.

Theory should not be discarded, but caution must be used in how a theory is implemented in treating real-life problems. In Chapter 2, it was pointed out that it is probable that the number of self-help groups is increasing in large part due to the fact that individuals seeking help are not finding it through the usual psychological channels. Rigid adherence to theory must certainly be playing a part in client dissatisfaction. The proper use of a theory requires that the practitioner carefully assess which parts of it are appropriate for the client's needs and which parts are not useful.

USING ESTABLISHED THEORETICAL APPROACHES

Because there is little information on many real-life problems, there is little information on the role of theory in helping people experiencing them. Thus, it is not possible to say whether one treatment approach is more useful than another in dealing with real-life problems. Moreover, it is difficult to envision the day when one approach will attain superiority over the others. Regardless, it really does not matter which approach is used as long as the clinician exhibits caution and careful deliberation about a theory's applicability in a specific situation. Research has repeatedly shown that no theoretical approach is superior to another in helping people presenting psychopathological problems (e.g., Smith, Glass, & Miller, 1980). Effective treatment depends more on who is offering the help than on which theory is being used. This conclusion certainly extends to dealing real-life problems.

It should come as no surprise that some clinicians are developing treatment approaches for real-life problems based on theories ranging from psychodynamic to behavioral. However, the developments have positive and negative aspects.

Perhaps of all the approaches, the psychodynamic theory group (e.g., Freudian theory), which emphasizes unconscious causes and symbolism, presents the greatest risk of being misapplied in real-life cases if the helper is not especially vigilant. The concern here is that a real-life problem may be construed in psychodynamic terms that are inaccurate. When one leaves the realm of fact and enters the world of the unconscious and symbolism, it is especially easy to find representations of "facts" because one is looking for them. For example, it would be easy to suggest that the long-term sadness a person feels is a result of unexpressed anger turned inward or the product of some unresolved childhood conflict, ignoring the rather obvious point that the sadness is clearly warranted due to the realities of a specific circumstance, such as the loss of family members in an auto accident. The misinterpretation by the therapist can be further perpetuated if the client should disagree with the therapist's misinterpretation, because the disagreement itself is seen as an interpretable sign of something deeper (e.g., resistance). (See Masson, 1988, and Sulloway, 1991.) Should this type of misunderstanding occur, it would be expected that the client would become frustrated and withdraw from further contacts with the therapist.

Of course, a real-life problem may well stir up deeper psychological concerns, but the helper must be careful not to interpret all concerns in this light. Horowitz (1974) has shown how a real-life situation may be a source of both realistic concerns and deeper psychological issues, such as the activation of a past conflict. The Horowitz article also reported an excellent approach to using psychodynamic theory in helping a person if it is reasonably and sensitively applied. Because of the potential for misinterpretation, psychodynamic diagnosticians and therapists must create in themselves a constant reminder that the client is not an interesting case of arrested development or the product of deep-seated, unresolved conflicts.

Humanistic (phenomenological) theories, which emphasize the client's unique self and view of the world, can be greatly suited to working with real-life problems if they are employed correctly. Because of the emphasis on understanding the unique person, and relative lack of emphasis on theoretical constructs, humanistic approaches can offer clients opportunities to freely explore real-life situations. Humanistic approaches strongly emphasize positive attitudes and self-growth potential. Thus, the primary caution to be exercised with this type of approach is to avoid the tendency to present an overly optimistic expectation that the client will be able to gain some kind of strength and self-growth from the experience. As an example of using a phenomenological approach, McCarthy, Reese, Schueneman, and Reese (1991) found the framework of Maslow's hierarchy of needs to be helpful in providing counseling to working class women.

The existential approach to helping is difficult to concisely define. As Fallon (1992) noted, "Existentialists are a diverse bunch. In fact, most of them object to being placed in the same classification with the others" (p. 1434). Most clinicians using an existentialist approach believe people must define their own purpose in life, find their own meaning in life's events, and be responsible for the choices they make (within the limits set by reality). For a number of reasons, this approach is well-suited to dealing with real-life problems. First, it focuses on the client's view of the situation. Second, it does not view the world in overly optimistic ways (i.e., it is realistic). Third, the client is encouraged to be authentic (not to deny who and what one is). This is important because it encourages the client to acknowledge and accept thoughts and feelings that other people might not understand. Kinzie and his colleagues (e.g., Kinzie & Fleck, 1987) have found the existential approach to be the most useful one in dealing with severely traumatized refugees.

Behavioral, specifically cognitive-behavioral, approaches emphasize the effects of a person's thought processes in causing, maintaining, and resolving psychological issues. In this context, helping involves helping a person alter maladaptive thinking (e.g., to stop focusing on negative events or consider an issue from another perspective). This approach has been effectively used with real-life problems, for example, in helping cancer patients deal with the effects of their illness (Golden, Gersh, & Robbins, 1992). The potential problem in using this approach with real-life problems is the tendency to psychologize all thinking in maladaptive terms and, as a result, misinterpret the problem and inappropriately attempt to alter the client's feelings and thoughts about the problem. A person undergoing a real-life problem is feeling and thinking in a logical, rational manner. As unpleasant as some thoughts, feelings, and memories may be, they are not in need of being altered: They are real, justified, and rational.

WHERE DOES THIS LEAVE THEORY?

As should be evident by now, two conclusions can be drawn about theories in general related to treating real-life problems. First, all theories offer some potential to be helpful in dealing with real-life problems. Second, all theories can be misused if they are adhered to in a rigid manner. Essentially, as would be true in treating for psychopathological problems, all theories have some potential, and no theory has all the answers for treating real-life problems.

Basically, when all is said and done, the value of a specific theory is really secondary to the importance of the personal qualities of the person helping someone with a real-life problem. Advocates of a specific approach may feel otherwise, but consider the work of George Kelly (1969). He wrote, "I began fabricating 'insights.' I deliberately offered 'preposterous' interpretations to my clients" (p. 52). Kelly found that even if an interpretation was contrived, it was helpful as long as it led to the client viewing himself or herself and the problems in a different way.

Kelly's work points to the difficulty in using theories with both psychopathological and real-life problems. It is clear that the clients will tend to accept an interpretation simply on the basis of the interpreter's authority. (Note the relevance of the work of Kaminer, 1992, Loftus, 1993, and Tavris, 1993.) Helpers must be exceedingly cautious about letting their theory control how a person's real-life situation is conceptualized and treated. There must be an ongoing process of self-monitoring to ensure that a client's concerns are seen through clear, objective, unbiased eyes.

4 WHAT IS NORMAL UNDER THE CIRCUMSTANCES?

Understanding and helping a person undergoing a real-life problem of either type requires knowledge of what is and is not normal under the specific circumstances. If some aspect of the individual's problems fall into the psychopathological category, traditional mental health treatment must be used in addressing that aspect. However, if the reactions of the person fall into the normal and expected category, measures aimed at the removal of psychopathological issues will be clearly inappropriate.

The line between normal and abnormal has never been clear. The concepts do not fit into neat, discrete categories, and this chapter is not meant to be an academic discussion of the concept of normality. An excellent presentation of the dimensions of normality is already available (Offer & Sabshin, 1966, 1974, 1984, 1991). Likewise, just what constitutes abnormality is readily found in any abnormal psychology textbook. The focus here is specifically on normal reactions that should be expected in a person undergoing a real-life problem.

Perhaps the single most important point to begin this discussion with is that there is no accepted definition of normal. What is or is not normal depends on one's culture and social class, the situation itself, and the theoretical orientation of the mental health person with whom one works, to name only a few of the influences.

In the greatest part of current mental health practice, the medical definition of health (i.e., the absence of sickness) is used to define mental health. This approach is reflected in the American Psychiatric Association's DSM

III-R (1987). Specifically, mental health is the absence of psychopathology. The tacit acknowledgment of this definition relieves us of the burden of having to list specific and definite criteria for normal. However, although this may be useful in dealing with mental illness, it is not especially helpful in dealing with normal reactions: It tells us what the person is not, not what the person is.

To understand and work with people with real-life problems, the helper must broaden his or her standard definition of what constitutes normality to cover the wide range of normality extending from people who are essentially stress-free and living happy, productive lives to those living with stresses and strains that are uncomfortable and unpleasant, but do not reach psychopathological proportions. Normal grieving is a good example of a person in deep emotional distress who is nonetheless perfectly normal. Clearly, what is normal may include very strong, distressing reactions. Under the conditions of real-life problems, overwhelming emotions such as sadness and worry are to be expected. They are normal under the circumstances.

The best guideline for deciding whether a person's psychological state is normal is an assessment of what a person's thoughts and emotions are doing to his or her life. This is the kind of everyday information any mental health professional would evaluate when asked, "Is it normal for...?" In the absence of specific criteria for normality, the worker must resort to a combination of common sense and professional judgment. If reactions to a real-life problem are creating no discernable deleterious effects for the client and other people around him or her, the term abnormal would be inappropriate. It is expected that strong feelings, intrusive thoughts, recurring reflections, and memories will occur. If a person continues to work, study, maintain personal relations, keep up a home, and in other ways function effectively, he or she would have to be considered normal.

Following the same line of reasoning, if the effects of a real-life event have begun to interfere with a person's ability to maintain effective, productive day-to-day living, if the person has become suicidal, or if the lives of others are being adversely affected, it is appropriate to consider that psychopathological problems are present. The diagnosis may fall under one or more than one diagnostic category. If psychopathology is present, the psychopathological aspects of the person's problem must be treated according to standard methods, and intervention must shift toward a more psychopathological mode. At the same time, the real-life aspects of the problem must be dealt with as such, not as another manifestation of psychopathological conditions. Of course, it is possible that a person undergoing a real-life problem will have periods when the effects are much greater than usual, resulting in transient psychopathological symptoms. Ordinary, day-to-day stress may be handled effectively by a person, but under the duress of added stresses, such as a death or sickness, the person's coping ability may be temporarily taxed beyond capacity. Kinzie and Fleck (1987) refer to this exacerbation as reactivation.

It should be evident that the expected reactions of a person undergoing a real-life problem must be seen as fluid, as waxing and waning. Real-life problems are unique situations with serious effects, and the profession must remain flexible and open to be able to deal effectively with them. Inversely, strong reactions must not be assumed to be psychopathological, even if they do press the limits of conventional ideas of normality.

In the context of this broader definition of normal, it is possible to consider the differences between normal effects and reactions associated with temporal problems (Chapter 5) and those associated with lasting real-life problems (Chapter 6). The delineation is not always clear because both types of problems share aspects of sadness, guilt, anger, and other emotions and responses. However, it is possible to examine the type, frequency, combination of reactions, and degree of effect, which will vary from person to person and over time within the same person. It cannot be emphasized too strongly that each person must be considered in light of his or her unique situation, and it is understood that expected reactions are to remain within the limits of normal.

A difficulty in the previous discussion lies in the fact that the issues appear to be so evident that discussion seems superfluous. Simple logic should tell us that the reactions and feelings most people experience during real-life problems are both natural and normal. At the same time, defining common aspects experienced in real-life problems permits us to establish a common understanding and lays the groundwork upon which we can build effective methods for helping.

5 NORMAL UNDER THE CIRCUMSTANCES: TEMPORAL REAL-LIFE PROBLEMS

This chapter discusses eight aspects of temporal real-life problems: domination of the problem; loss of control; depression; cycling of hope and despair; anger, resentment, and frustration; overreaction; anxiety; and guilt. Individuals may experience other emotions and reactions unique to them or shared by only a few other people. However, these eight aspects are typical of most people enduring a temporal real-life problem.

DOMINATION OF THE PROBLEM OVER THE PERSON

The person undergoing a situation of the magnitude described in this book comes to be dominated by the situation. This reflects the fact that the situation demands the attention of the person. To the helper, this domination of the person by the problem may appear to be a manifestation of the person's inability to "let go" of the problem. However, this is not obsessiveness, with its connotation of psychopathology. As noted previously, the problem will not let go of the person. The day-to-day worries about a parent or child, the worries about how one will get food, or the ever present fear of a medical crisis simply do not allow the person the option to set the problem aside. The person is preoccupied with the situation because there is no choice. Making frequent references to the situation reflects the depth of concern and fear the person is experiencing, not some hidden desire to hold on to the situation.

LOSS OF CONTROL OVER ONE'S LIFE

It will often be the case that a person with a temporal real-life problem will feel he or she has no control over life. There is a valid perception that life is being controlled by someone or something else. At least, the events virtually require a constant devotion of attention to the problems being generated by some outside force. For example, once one is involved in the legal system, matters seem to take on a life of their own. If a loved one is very ill, there is little the helper can do to change the situation. If a child, a brother. or a sister is out of control, the parent or relative becomes a recipient of the negative effects of whatever is done by the other person. To say that one is able to take charge of one's own life rather naively ignores the fact that life consists of dealing with and reacting to other people and situations that impose themselves on unwilling persons.

DEPRESSION

Given the nature of the circumstances that produce real-life problems, depression is to be expected. After all, the person is caught in a situation of immense proportions. It is depressing to feel that life is out of control. There may be the pain of separation, of lost hopes or dreams, of ongoing emotional storms. The level of depression will rise and fall as would be expected in any situation, but the person will continue on in spite of the depression.

CYCLES OF HOPE AND DESPAIR

The person will go through periods where hope rises that the situation will somehow abate, only to be reminded that the hope was not justified. The rebellious child who shows a renewed interest in the family raises hopes only to dash them by another rebellious act. The accused person reads something that causes a sense of hope, only to be sent another legal document reminding her or him of the true situation. A letter is received from an estranged relative, only an attempt to make contact with the person results in further rebuff. The cycle may repeat itself many times, with increasingly marked high and low points of emotion.

ANGER, RESENTMENT, AND FRUSTRATION

Feelings of anger, resentment, and frustration are normal as the individual deals with the fact that life seems to have gone out of its way to inflict pain and to put roadblocks in the way of resolving anything. The actions of others may warrant anger. A person's ability to act may be limited by time, resources, knowledge, access to help, or because there are literally no alternatives available. The financial ruin, the emotional pain inflicted by someone, the consequences of careless or thoughtless actions — these and other events will generate anger, resentment, and frustration.

OVERREACTION

The person is very likely to overreact to situations that relate to the temporal real-life problem. The person will be worn threadbare emotionally by the situation and will expect more of the same. Essentially, the person develops a kind of siege mentality because she or he has learned not to let his or her guard down. The person comes to expect unpredictable difficulty. Although no harm is intended or even evident, relatively minor situations may lead to a person overreacting. For example, a relative's casual remark may be taken wrongly or a child's innocent behavior may be taken as a sign of disrespect or manipulation.

ANXIETY

In the presence of unpredictable circumstances and seemingly uncontrollable events, it is natural for a person to experience anxiety or worry. How could it be otherwise, given the situation? Any person would be anxious under such circumstances. The person is perhaps facing a ruined reputation, job loss, or jail time. The situation may involve expecting to hear some very bad news about a child or spouse being arrested or receiving a serious medical diagnosis. Moreover, the anxiety is heightened in that in most cases there is no way to anticipate how long the situation is going to continue. There are no specified final points that allow the person to feel he or she is working toward an end to the situation. The person keeps asking how long he or she will be trapped in the situation, but there are no answers.

GUILT

A person of conscience accepts the standards and criteria used for evaluating behaviors in his or her social unit. When through action or inaction, by choice or chance, that person causes harm, the person is likely to feel guilty. Because people tend to be self-critical, much of the guilt they feel is not really warranted, but not all guilt is irrational (Potter-Effron, 1987). Guilt is not always a pathological distortion of conscience. In some cases, having feelings of guilt is natural; that is, the person did or did not do something that realistically resulted in feelings of guilt. For example, a person may take a foolish financial risk that fails, resulting in the impoverishment of his or her family. Out of anger, a person may say something to another person that results in estrangement, or take risks that result in serious health problems, or knowingly behave carelessly, resulting in injury to another person. In each case, it is normal for a person of conscience to feel guilt; such feelings are not irrational.

6 NORMAL UNDER THE CIRCUMSTANCES: LASTING REAL-LIFE PROBLEMS

Although there is a general lack of recognition of the need to address real-life problems, in comparison with lasting real-life problems, temporal real-life problems are more likely to be understood by helpers and to have more written about them. Consider the number of books on crisis counseling and the numerous articles written about acute distress, both normal and not-normal. Lasting real-life problems require special attention, even beyond that required to understand and treat temporal real-life problems. Although there is a fair amount of overlap between normal characteristics and manifestations of the two types of problems, lasting real-life problems are marked by a difference in the *quality* of a person's reactions.

It must be kept in mind that a lasting real-life problem is a reaction to a past event that has left the person altered for life. The origin of the problem might lie in what was formerly a temporal problem, and events may have qualified as posttraumatic stress disorders at one time. However, lasting real-life problems envelope a person long after the immediate situation has been addressed, perhaps years or decades later. Lasting real-life problems are commonly characterized by seven components: sadness, guilt, anxiety, anger and resentment, reflection, reactivation, and longevity.

SADNESS

It could be argued that sadness and depression are interchangeable terms. However, sadness associated with lasting real-life problems is unlikely to be maintained over long periods of time at a level of severity that would warrant describing it as serious depression. This kind of sadness has a quality different from that of what we think of as depression. It is marked less by active symptoms (e.g., crying, physical distress) than by what the person senses to be an emotional void. One of the more common descriptions of the sadness associated with lasting real-life problems is that a person's sense of joy and enthusiasm about life have been diminished. There is a nagging feeling that something precious has been taken away and will never be returned, that complete happiness is no longer possible.

The inadequacy of this description reflects the difficulty of trying to convey feelings through words. Those who have had and are experiencing this condition will immediately recognize it, even if these words fail to convey the nature and depth of the feeling to readers who have not experienced such sadness. It is important for the helper to recognize that people who are experiencing this type of sadness are not in a psychopathological depression. In fact, many people with real-life problems do not use the words, "I am depressed." Rather, they state their feelings in terms of what is not being felt. It is not that the person is completely devoid of the ability to laugh and feel happiness. Rather, it is just that a sadness exists underneath every experience of joy and pleasure. This sense of sadness pervades the person's life and becomes a constant companion.

ANXIETY

Anxiety associated with lasting real-life problems is best described as a generalized sense of being unsettled and uncertain about life. A number of words other than anxiety could be used, for example, dread, worry, uncertainty, and fear. This anxiety is based in the person's real-life lesson that life is not always fair, that it does not always make sense, and that the rules of life are not as clear and predictable as he or she once believed. Once a person learns this difficult lesson, that person has an ever-present recognition that another event like the event that created his or her distress could happen again. Just because life has thrown a person a curve once does not mean it cannot happen again. It is all too clear that life follows its own rules, not ours.

A person who is experiencing either a temporal or lasting real-life problem has reason to be anxious about the future. However, the person who experiences a temporal real-life problem still has time to hope matters will be resolved, however depressed he or she may feel from time to time. The person experiencing a lasting real-life problem has reason to know that future resolution is not possible. The rules of life she or he once believed have been thrown into permanent disarray. Unalterable events have occurred. Parents are supposed to die before their children, but their child died first. A person has been taught and believes that hard work, honesty, and integrity insure job and financial security, but is fired just before he or she reaches retirement age. Post-retirement years are supposed to be golden years, a time of relaxation and contentment, only a very serious illness devours one's savings and destroys one's health. When such events occur, people become apprehensive because life is not supposed to work that way, and it is no longer clear how and why life works the way it does. As it is, all a person knows for sure is that nothing is certain — a lesson about life that he or she would gladly forfeit, if that were possible.

GUILT

As noted in previous chapters, although much of the guilt and shame people feel is not realistically warranted, feelings of guilt and shame are not always irrational, nor is guilt necessarily a distortion of one's conscience. Rather, in some circumstances, feelings of guilt may be rational and warranted (Potter-Effron, 1987). Moreover, feelings of guilt are unavoidable for a person of conscience. In fact, if a person does not feel guilt when it is appropriate, there is cause for concern. Examples of circumstances in which feelings of guilt are warranted and rational include causing a fatal automobile accident when driving while intoxicated, permanently injuring someone by the reckless use of machinery, and destroying another person's life through one's own egocentric needs and demands.

It is not likely to ease the pain to any significant degree to tell the person that he or she did not intend to cause harm, that what happened was not his or her fault. Such comforting underestimates the self-understanding of the person, who knows better. It is equally inappropriate to suggest to the person that the guilt is a product of some irrational or unwarranted thought pattern, of an overactive superego or social conscience, when the fact is that the guilt is based on that person's accurate assessment of his or her involvement in the situation and the permanence of its effects.

To couch the guilt in psychopathological terms is to deny the truth and to deny the person's justified suffering. To deny the guilt and its source is equivalent to denying a very real part of the person's life or, in existential terms, to try to force the person to be inauthentic (untrue to oneself). A person simply cannot deny an emotion of such great significance—unpleasant and unfortunate though it may be, the emotion is nonetheless reality. The person in pain is more likely to benefit from knowing that another person acknowledges the pain and understands it, rather than from being pressured to deny it.

ANGER AND RESENTMENT

Certain real-life events are especially fertile ground for creating anger and resentment. A person who has been brutalized has cause to feel anger toward the perpetrator. Having spent all possible energy to get a loved one to quit a health-endangering habit, a person may be expected to feel anger when the loved one dies at a young age or throws the family into bankruptcy because of massive medical bills that could have been avoided. Anger should be expected when a person sees a loved one on a collision course with destruction, such as using drugs or engaging in criminal activity, and does everything possible to help the loved one only to have the situation end tragically. Having one's life destroyed by the willful actions of another person can do little else than create anger. Expending every effort to change a negative situation and failing time and again can only lead to frustration.

Anger is a difficult emotion for many people to handle, even under the best of circumstances. Under the effects of a lasting real-life problem, it is even more difficult. The anger, irrespective of its being justified, will collide with other feelings such as love, concern, and compassion. Of course, in turn, the feelings of anger help produce guilt for the person feeling the anger.

REFLECTION

The person undergoing a lasting real-life problem will continue to pour over and reflect upon the event or events that brought it all about. Reflecting on and perhaps even reliving the event likely are unavoidable. The degree of emotion during these periods of reflection will vary and is probably related to the degree of trauma at the time of the event. For example, see Kinzie and Fleck (1987), van der Veer (1992), and Mollica (1988) for discussions of severely traumatized refugees. Also, see Eaton, Signal, and Weinfield (1982) and Mattussek (1975) for discussions of surviving the Holocaust.

REACTIVATION

In a study of traumatized refugees, Kinzie and Fleck (1987) noted that the refugees experienced posttraumatic exacerbations of emotions and memories, which were triggered by a wide variety of events ranging from those clearly related to their experience (e.g., a news story about the event) to events less obviously connected (e.g., children moving away). Kinzie and Fleck referred to this phenomenon as reactivation.

It is reasonable to assume that other lasting real-life problems would be subject to reactivation. In fact, reactivation is common in those experiencing lasting real-life problems. Apparently innocuous events may arouse emotions as deep as open discussion of the event. Reactivation may be disconcerting to both client and helper if it is not recognized as being normal under the circumstances. A sudden welling up of emotion must not be considered a sign of weakening psychological strength.

LONGEVITY

People with lasting real-life problems endure the effects of the problem in varying degrees for the rest of their lives. For example, see Lukas and Seiden (1990), Masters, Friedman, and Gretzel (1988), and Rando (1986) for discussions about long-term effects of different kinds of precipitating events. Time will not heal such problems. Recall Rynearson's comment: "I and other survivors can never be 'cured' in the sense of being restored, for suicide represents a life change that literally 'changes' one" (1981, p. 86). There is no light at the end of the tunnel. The most important point to acknowledge about longevity is that the person does not hold on to the problem out of some psychopathological need to punish herself or himself or from some deep-seated need to suffer. Again, the person is not holding on to the problem; rather, the problem is holding on to the person. The person would gladly let go of the pain if that were possible. However, some events are so overwhelming they simply cannot be put in the past, and the person must continually deal with the pain. Shakespeare succinctly described this condition in *King John* (Act 3, Scene 4), when Constance says:

> I am not mad, I would to heaven I were!
> For then 'tis like I should forget myself:
> O, if I could, what grief should I forget! (p. 362)

In general, the effects of a lasting real-life problem can be summarized in the words "life-altering." Life will never be the same for this individual. All the helper can do is to help the person learn to live with the pain and to go on in spite of it.

7   GUIDELINES FOR HELPING

Helping people with real-life problems calls for flexibility because of the large number of possible precipitating events and the highly individual nature of a person's reactions to an event (e.g., Everstine & Everstine, 1993; Kennedy, 1981). As is true in any helping relationship, helping must be tailored to the specific needs of the individual. Some individuals may be more saddened than anxious, while others may be predominantly guilt-ridden. Successful intervention depends on two factors: an appropriate therapeutic attitude and flexibility in choosing and using methods of helping.

CHANGES IN THERAPEUTIC ATTITUDE

It is not an exaggeration to state that for the typical mental health worker to be able to help a person with a real-life problem, the helper's attitude about treatment must undergo a major shift. Most helpers must discard or at least alter many of the beliefs and guidelines that work well with psychopathological disorders. It is not that there are no models for helping with real-life problems (e.g., rehabilitation, medical psychology), rather, it is the case that the typical mental health worker is not familiar with those models. Specifically, there are four areas in which changes are required: conceptualizing the problem, establishing the length of time for the helping process, setting goals for effective intervention, and defining success in treatment.

Conceptualizing the problem

In dealing with a psychopathological problem, it is generally helpful to conceptualize the situation in terms of a theoretical framework. Whether the helper uses an established framework (e.g., psychodynamics) or an eclectic approach, both helper and client benefit if the theory is used appropriately. Understanding is enhanced, and established treatment guidelines and techniques are suggested. However, conceptualizing a real-life problem and its treatment is another matter.

Because people with real-life problems are reacting to an overwhelming situation that actually exists, the use of standard theoretical approaches can become problematical. Using currently available theories leads to the tendency to conceptualize a real-life problem only in terms that are better suited to psychopathological disorders. As a result, it is almost certain that the client's behavior, thoughts, and emotions will be misconstrued. To suggest that a client's reaction results from the person being inauthentic, is a manifestation of unresolved childhood conflicts, originates in a conflict between primary and secondary drives, or is a result of a lack of secondary reinforcers from the environment is to deny the simple reality of the person's situation. To repeat a quotation used earlier, Kennedy (1981) said, "Yet another sign of this is the determined efforts on the part of some helpers to apply a model of counseling whether it fits or not" (p. 22).

Most helpers do not feel the need to develop a comprehensive theory to explain depression over the death of a spouse, parent, or child. They do not spend a great deal of time developing theoretical explanations of why a person wants to live in a home, go to the grocery store, or talk to a friend. Some emotions, thoughts, and behaviors simply do not require further explanation. Nor is it necessary when treating real-life problems to develop a psychological interpretation of why a person is saddened, angry, guilt ridden, or worried. There is no need for a psychological theory to explain why the problem will not go away. The causes, reactions, and longevity are obvious.

Length of the Helping Process

It is generally understood, with only occasional exceptions, that traditional psychotherapy is time-limited, especially with today's increasing emphasis on brief therapy. Regardless of the anticipated length of treatment time for psychopathological disorders, it is understood that at some point therapy will be terminated, because the problem has been resolved. However, real-life problems do not have a clearly defined ending point. Even in the case of a temporal real-life problem, which offers hope of resolution, how long the problem will go on is uncertain, and it is quite likely that even after the ongoing situation has passed, there will be sequelae with which the person and the helper must deal.

In the case of lasting real-life problems, it is certain that there will be no resolution; thus, there can be no definable end-point to helping. Helpers who work with chronic serious psychological disorders, including the distress associated with lasting real-life problems, recognize the need for prolonged intervention. Professionals such as Werth and Oseroff (1987), who worked with families of disabled children, and Kinzie and Fleck (1987), who worked with traumatized refugees, think that treatment must be an ongoing process, perhaps enduring the lifetime of the client.

Helping a person with a real-life problem requires a long-term commitment on the part of the helper. Dealing with problems that have no end can become frustrating and discouraging for the helper and can create resentment toward the client. However, protracted intervention does not necessarily mean weekly sessions; in fact, it would be surprising if such intense treatment was necessary in most cases. It is more likely that the client will require varying amounts of help. During anniversary times or other events that exacerbate the real-life problem, the need for help will be greater. Thus, help must be offered on an as-needed basis.

The Goal of Helping

In treating psychopathological disorders, the goal (ignoring differences across theories) is to uncover the problem, confront it, and resolve it. If this process is successful, the client will continue forward, having left the problem in the past. This is not the case with real-life problems. Not only is there a lack of possibility for resolution, there is no problem to be uncovered. Trying to confront the person's problem may well be the worst therapeutic approach that could be taken.

The goal of helping with a real-life problem is effective maintenance, not cure. Psychological maintenance is directly equivalent to treating a chronic medical condition such as diabetes. Diabetes is not curable, but the patient can lead an otherwise healthy, productive, long life if proper medical attention is obtained and the treatment regime is followed. Without denying the impact of the precipitating or ongoing event, the person with a real-life problem can learn to assimilate the emotional pain into his or her overall life style.

As Kinzie and Fleck (1987) noted, "For many, if not most, a cure is not possible; there is no way to integrate the past and go on with life as before" (p 91). Eaton, Signal, and Weinfield (1982) reported that 33 years after the Holocaust, survivors reported more psychiatric symptoms than controls (even though the survivors had otherwise successfully gone on with life). Norton (1989) presented many case descriptions of people who would clearly qualify as having a real-life problem, but who also continued to live effectively. Reissman (1985) noted, "In many cases, of course, these stressors cannot be eliminated or reduced by the individual. Illness or death of a loved one, accidents, and economic setbacks are not easily controllable and in some cases impossible to control" (p. 3). It must be remembered that the goal of helping with real-life problems is to help the individual maintain as effective an adjustment as the prevailing conditions allow. The practical aim is to assist the person to lead the most productive, satisfying life possible under the circumstances.

Defining Success in Helping

All people like to feel they are successful. It is difficult to maintain enthusiasm for what one is doing if one confronts continued failure or at least minimal experiences with success. It follows that if the goals of helping with real-life problems are different from the usual treatment goals, then the definition of success will also be different. Success in helping with real-life problems must be defined along two related criteria. First, if the client continues to seek help rather than discontinuing treatment, part of the definition of success has been met. The client has maintained contact with the helper, which implies that something beneficial is occurring.

Second, the helper must consider how well the person is able to continue effective adjustment in spite of the real-life problem. This is directly analogous to working with chronic mental illness, wherein success is defined as the client staying out of the hospital, establishing at least minimal social involvement, maintaining employment, or living independently and relatively free of disturbing symptoms. Although these outcomes would be rather minimal for treatment of many other psychological disorders, they are quite appropriate for the chronic client. The helper must give up the idea of success meaning a client has addressed and resolved concerns to the point that they no longer hamper the individual's life. Any helper who tries to use these criteria of success will inevitably experience failure. So it is in treating real-life problems.

METHODS OF HELPING

The ways in which help can be offered are varied, and the helper must keep an open mind about the best way to proceed. Psychotherapy may or may not be the best treatment, the mental health worker may not be the best person to offer help, and methods that are not usually viewed as mental health techniques must be considered. Referral may be not only desirable, but necessary.

The discussion that follows is not a comprehensive discussion of specific techniques. No new techniques are offered. It is not a review of the literature on the effectiveness of the various techniques. The purpose of the discussion is to present treatment possibilities, not to prescribe the specific manner in which treatment should be conducted. The list of helping techniques is not in any order of importance or preference. The only inflexible guidelines for helping with real-life problems are to use whatever works and to refer the person to a more appropriate helper if such skills are not in one's repertoire.

Psychotherapy

In the context of this discussion, the term psychotherapy is being used in a very general sense to refer to both traditional and behavioral approaches. The differences between behavioral and non-behavioral treatments are not important for the purposes of this discussion. However, effective use of psychotherapy in treating real-life problems requires a shift in thinking on the part of the helper. Of course, for any intervention, certain basic therapeutic skills could be used, such as being a good listener, being unconditionally supportive, allowing the client to set the tone for discussions, developing and expressing empathy, and having knowledge of the person's situation. However, some of the time-honored tools used in psychotherapy may not be appropriate with real-life problems. In fact, some of the traditional techniques are directly opposite to the techniques that are likely to help.

Kinzie and Fleck (1987), in treating severely traumatized refugees, suggested that therapists should not expect an outpouring of emotions from the client. Trauma will leave the person emotionally numb for years after the event, and very likely the numbness will be permanent. (Among others, also see Mollica, 1988, and van der Veer, 1992). The numbing can reasonably be expected in varying degrees with other real-life problems. Either the event will be so overwhelming that the person will be rendered numb, or the person will have already spent his or her emotions and will have come to the point that further expression seems futile. Numbing is less likely with temporal real-life problems, but it is quite likely that the person will reach a feeling of futility about the value of further discussion. Eventually, the client will realize that what could be said has already been said over and over again.

The numbness and sense of futility must not be interpreted as apathy or indifference. Rather, they are clear indicators of the degree of the person's pain. Although White (1964) found that expression of emotion is a common factor across all psychotherapies, this is not always possible for people with real-life problems and is probably not beneficial (unless the client feels the need to talk about emotions). The client must not be coerced to express feelings, thoughts, or memories in the mistaken belief that such catharsis is automatically beneficial. The client will decide this for himself or herself.

Contrary to much of what psychotherapists have been taught about helping people, the purpose of treating real-life problems may not be to get the client to bring out troubling thoughts and emotions. The goal may be much more pragmatic. The helper must answer a single question in order to decide how to proceed: "Will bringing out this material serve any useful purpose?" In the case of very severe trauma, the therapist may actively encourage the client not to confront the issue. This is not to say the client should deny the event (How could he or she deny it?), only that a continued reworking of the events will serve no therapeutic purpose. Kinzie and Fleck (1987) noted with traumatized refugees, "It is generally advisable to support psychiatric suppression and avoidance behaviors that are part of the syndrome and probably adaptive" (p. 92). Discussing coping with medical illness, Miller (1992) stated, "Maintaining a sense of normalcy includes keeping signs and symptoms under control or out of view of persons surrounding the individual" (p. 27). This is not so far removed from what therapists tell chronically mentally ill persons: "Control your behavior, act in a socially appropriate manner, and go on living in spite of your symptoms."

Client avoidance of discussion must not be interpreted as evidence of psychopathological threat or resistance to treatment that must be worked through. Given the client's situation, he or she is coping in the best way possible. There must be no expectation, direct or implied, that the client must deal with issues the therapist has defined as necessary. Such exploration by the client is appropriate only when it will accomplish something for the client. How many times must the client discuss something that is not really resolvable? In her work with dying people, Kubler-Ross (1969) noted that sometimes the only therapy needed is to sit quietly with the person. Kinzie and Fleck (1987) wrote, "At times there is nothing to say or do but just to sit with the patient in silent companionship. . . . In the end, no words can heal and at times nothing can be added to what has been done or said" (p. 88).

Helping with real-life problems may well call for greater therapist involvement than is usually considered necessary or desirable by the therapist. Discussing working with clients experiencing chronic serious mental illness, Rappaport et al. (1985) noted how psychotherapists and other mental health workers resist changing their roles to be more helpful to clients: "We found they were often unwilling to give up control over the lives of their patients, and yet were unavailable other than at regularly scheduled meeting times or during an extreme crisis, and then almost always in their office. They were in no sense a part of the client's day-to-day effective support network..." (p. 14). The same authors went on to say, "Mental health professionals are by and large unwilling, and perhaps unable, to do what is necessary to create the kinds of day-to-day support systems needed" (p. 14). Kubler-Ross (1969) noted that helping the dying requires being there when the person needs help, not when it is convenient for the helper.

Helping people with real-life problems does not require deep-seated psychotherapy; there are no deep problems to be addressed and resolved. Rather, helping with real-life problems falls into the supportive and educative categories. The particular theory a helper uses is not critical, as noted earlier, and whether or not helping should be individual or in a group is a matter to be decided in each case. If groups are to be used, it is strongly advised that the participants share a common real-life problem. For example, a person who was directly responsible for a number of deaths and a person whose child is in prison both have real-life problems, but the situations are different enough that the two people are unlikely to attain more than partial understanding of each other's situation.

The course of real-life problems is usually sporadic, and the emotional and psychological storm intensifies and lessens. Thus, the client will seek help on a periodic basis. In other words, the helper should not anticipate the typical one-hour-per-week schedule for therapy. Flexibility in scheduling is required. Regularly scheduled sessions may actually work against the client returning as she or he becomes uncomfortable in sessions where discussion is expected but is neither necessary nor useful to the client.

Using psychotherapy in helping with a real-life problem involves three basic therapeutic principles. First, the person's pain must be acknowledged as the result of a real-life situation. The person needs to be assured of the normality of what he or she is experiencing, that she or he is not overreacting or losing psychological control.

Second, the helper must acknowledge with the person that the problem is not curable. If the client is to gain benefit from the sessions, she or he must hear the therapist acknowledge what the client already knows: The problem is overwhelming and not reversible. Even in the case of a temporal real-life problem, no assurances of resolution can be offered. This is not an especially pleasant message, but it is a truthful one.

The third basic principle is to offer support to the client and advice about ways to minimize the pain. The pain cannot be removed, but its intensity can perhaps be diminished. If the person has come to the point that talking about concerns is no longer useful, the therapist and client must work together to identify and use other methods (e.g., those presented later in this chapter). Because there are options, there is a legitimate message of hope that can be extended to the client.

Finally, it is also important to address interpersonal relations in the client's life, to involve family members and significant others in helping the client. Ongoing stresses present a very real possibility for strained relations with other people, and the client must be alert to this to prevent the strain from becoming destructive. Family therapy can reduce the strains of dealing with a real-life problem, as well as provide additional support in helping the client. In their work with physically disabled and chronically ill children, Sargent and Lieberman (1985) noted the importance of working with the family as well as with the child. Also, in most instances, families are involved in the treatment of clients during chronic mental illness.

Expressive Therapies

The term expressive therapies is commonly used to collectively describe techniques such as art therapy, dance therapy, and music therapy. The use of these expressive techniques must not be overlooked, either as part of an overall helping regimen or as the sole source of help. When words fail, expressive therapies present an attractive and useful option, for example, when the original trauma was so profound that words cannot be used to describe it. Expressive techniques allow revelations for both the client and the helper and offer emotional and psychological relief that words oftentimes cannot provide.

Given that expressive therapies are a form of mental health diagnosis and treatment, they are subject to the same precautions as were presented for psychotherapy. Expressive therapies are driven by various theories and can be misused as readily as any other form of treatment.

Self-Help Groups

Because real-life problems stem from a wide variety of events, there is no way any one helper could possibly know about the experiences, after-effects, and appropriate approaches in addressing all real-life problems. A helper's lack of knowledge and experience about a client's situation will be readily apparent to the client once treatment begins. This makes self-help groups an attractive option. As discussed in Chapter 2, the rapid rise in numbers of people using self-help — nearly 7 million a year — may demonstrate dissatisfaction with traditional treatment options. Regardless, self-help groups, if carefully selected based on the nature of the group and its participants' common experiences, may provide a person with both support and a source of alternatives for coping with pain and distress associated with real-life problems. (See also Gartner & Reissman, 1979; Jacobs & Goodman, 1989; Katz, 1981; Kurtz, 1990; Levy, 1976; Lieberman, 1986; Powell, 1987; and Rappaport et al., 1985.)

Some self-help groups encourage the involvement of mental health workers, while others are conducted by people who have experienced or are experiencing the particular problems on which the group is focussing. In address real-life problems, it does not matter who conducts a group, because the binding component of the group is that people who are participating share a common experience, are better able to understand how other participants feel, and have knowledge of the problems those feelings generate. Thus, self-help groups are especially appealing as a helping method for people with real-life problems.

It is understood that the mental health worker must be informed about a particular self-help group before referring a client to one. As Kaminer (1992) has cautioned, there is always the potential for these groups to be harmful as well as helpful (e.g., group leaders and techniques may promote dependency on the group, the regime may foster the notion that a person must confront an issue to be able to recover from it). As is true of therapists, not all self-help groups are equally effective.

Religion

As Kushner (1989), Peck (1978), and others have pointed out, the situations that create a real-life problem can create spiritual crises as the person struggles with the meaning of the events. Of course, not all people will have a spiritual crisis. However, if there is a spiritual concern, whether or not a specific helper feels qualified to deal with spiritual issues is an individual matter. In general, most mental health workers are not trained in theological matters and are unable to deal with specific spiritual issues (e.g., the client may be experiencing guilt because he or she adheres to a specific religious belief or because of a certain passage in a religious book).

Moreover, mental health workers are no more or less religious or faithful in attending religious services than their clients might be. Bergin and Jensen (1990) found that of 425 psychotherapists, 340 (80%) expressed a religious preference and 175 (41%) regularly attended religious services. Thus, both clients and most of their potential helpers are not likely to be prepared for serious discussions about religious matters. The concern here is not with the general struggling with belief, but with *specific* religious issues that the client may need to discuss. If the therapist is not qualified, referral must be made to an appropriately trained individual (which, of course, does not preclude the helper continuing to work with the client on other matters).

Literature

The use of fictional and nonfictional literature for therapeutic purposes is generally called bibliotherapy. (This discussion does not include so-called pop psychology books as sources of help, which will be discussed in detail in Chapter 8). Any reader of Shakespeare, Tolstoy, Dickens, or Hugo, for example, knows how well the human condition can be captured by a skilled writer. Bibliotherapy is an established source of help, with recent resources being readily available (e.g., Lerner & Mahlendorf, 1991; Miller, 1992; Pardek & Pardek, 1992). In most cases, the helper has the client read a piece of literature in order to provide a vehicle for discussion between the client and the helper. However, there is certainly no reason to believe that reading in and of itself cannot be therapeutic. Clearly, the client must decide if he or she desires discussion.

Not only can the client benefit from appropriate readings, but so can the helper. A helper can learn about a real-life problem in only three ways: by actually living through it, by working with people who have experienced it, and by learning about it through reading and other media experiences. In the end, no helper can share all experience directly, but being exposed to a variety of literature and other sources will help him or her to more easily recognize the commonality of experience for the client and others who have experienced similar real-life problems.

Stress Management

Stress management is an all-encompassing term for a wide variety of techniques intended to help reduce stress to manageable levels or eliminate it altogether. Common stress reduction techniques include relaxation training (including biofeedback), environmental changes to reduce stress, imagery, exercise, and time management. In addition, there are other tools, such as meditation (see Smith, 1986), which can aid in stress reduction.

There are many books on stress management for the helper not familiar with such techniques (e.g., Cotton, 1990; Patel, 1991; Peper & Holt, 1992). Moreover, seminars, books, programs, and classes on stress management abound. As is the case with self-help programs, the helper must be cautious about referral for stress management training if he or she is not familiar with a provider or a program.

Medication

Psychiatric medications should be considered if the person's emotional state is causing enough difficulty to warrant them. For example, if a person is losing sleep due to depression over the death of a loved one and is, therefore, unable to work, some form of short-term medication with antidepressants might be considered, However, for most people, medication will not be necessary, and it is best to avoid it if at all possible. Medications can sometimes cause as much harm as good, but if they are needed, the helper should not hesitate to recommend them.

Anything Else That Works For the Client

Mental health workers must be open quite literally to anything that will help the client find relief from her or his lasting storm. The client may find relief through a distraction—taking up a hobby, getting or changing a job, going to school, exercising, or traveling. One should not overlook the therapeutic use of laughter, as a number of writers have suggested (e.g., Cousins, 1979; Lefcourt & Martin, 1986; Morreall, 1983; Ziv, 1984). Temporary respite from the ongoing strain is a perfectly reasonable goal under the circumstances.

When selecting a helping option, the person's personality and the demands of the situation must be considered. Recommending a hobby to someone who has no interest in acquiring one will serve no purpose.

Suggesting that a person who has always been somewhat humorless should subject himself or herself to a long series of comedy sketches is unlikely to prove beneficial. If quiet contemplation with accompanying music works for the client, who is the helper to suggest otherwise? There is no established set of correct coping mechanisms, any more than there is a single correct theory about helping people.

THE ANSWER

In the end, helping a person with real-life problems requires creativity and flexibility. The helping regimen must be molded to the needs of the person, not the client to the method. Traditional techniques must be modified or suspended, and techniques not usually considered within the realm of mental health must be open as options.

8 AVOIDING POTENTIAL PROBLEMS IN HELPING

Clearly, helping a person with a real-life problem can be difficult for the helper because there are few specific rules about how to do it. If nothing else, it is important to learn what may actively work against helping the person. Simply stated, if there is a lack of certainty about what direction to follow, at least there is the obligation to minimize the potential misdirection. As noted in Chapter 2, empirical studies on treatment methods, efficacy, and potential problems do not exist; there are only those general guidelines provided in this volume and in a few other sources previously cited. However, practice in other areas and common sense have demonstrated a number of guidelines for what not to do, some of which have been alluded to earlier. This chapter summarizes the pitfalls to be avoided.

MAKING PSYCHOPATHOLOGICAL INTERPRETATIONS

Real-life problems may well involve strong emotions, longevity of concerns, and other emotional states that could easily be misinterpreted as signs of psychopathology. For example, justifiable guilt may be erroneously viewed by the helper as a manifestation of irrational self-punishment. The fact that the client cannot escape the real-life problem could easily be misinterpreted as the person not "wanting" to let go.

Psychopathological interpretations offer tempting answers and, in some cases, may be partially true for a person. Still, the psychopathological must be separated from the normal. Couching a person's condition in psychopathological terms when it is inappropriate creates two rather obvious problems. First, it misdirects the helping process. Second, it conveys to the client that he or she is clearly being misunderstood. Unfortunately, most clients would not confront a helper with the misinterpretation, because the helper has authority due to his or her professional role and status. It is more likely that the client will simply stop coming for help. The word "resent" may be strong, but resentment is a common reaction among people whose real-life situations and reactions have been interpreted as signs of psychopathology.

ALLOWING THEORY TO CONTROL THE PROCESS

It is crucial that the helper not allow a theoretical approach to drive the course of understanding and helping. This is as much of a mistake as interpreting normal reactions in psychopathological terms. For example, a cornerstone of the "systems" approach is to involve the whole interacting system, not simply the identified client. This may be appropriate in some cases, but in others it could easily drive the client away. What if, for the sake of argument, a person undergoing a real-life problem prefers to keep it quite literally personal? Perhaps the person does not care to "share" the pain with anyone else. The point applies to all theories. Techniques such as catharsis, confrontation, working through, and personal growth are theory-driven and may well be inappropriate with real-life problems.

ASSUMING A PARTICULAR TECHNIQUE IS BEST

Helpers tend to be enthusiastic about the techniques they use for understanding and helping others. With real-life problems, no technique can be categorically assumed to be the right or best one. The best one is the one that is suited to the individual needs of the client and his or her unique situation. Psychotherapy is not necessarily the best approach for all clients any more than art therapy or reading would be. A particular combination of techniques is not necessarily better suited to helping than is another combination.

For a helper to admit that he or she does not have the answers for the person and that favored theory and techniques are not likely to help can be threatening, and it is not usually easy to do so—but it is honest. Wolman (1976) noted, "Megalomania seems to be the main mental health hazard of psychotherapists. Many a psychiatrist or psychologist develops the illusion of omnipotence because the patient's glowing remarks and admiration can make him believe he possesses superhuman powers" (p. 16). There is no doubt about the need (and ethical requirement) to admit, if necessary, that help cannot be provided or that other types of intervention are more likely to be of benefit. Acknowledging the inability to help and referring the person to another source is a sign of competence, not an admission of failure.

JUDGING BY USUAL STANDARDS

Almost every person who has been subjected to a severe real-life trauma will never be the same. This is the nature of real-life problems, and it cannot be changed irrespective of how much we would like to do so. Dealing with the problem may require coping mechanisms that are out of the ordinary. If a person has found a way to control the situation and manage the stress, assuming there are no harmful effects to self and others, why should a helper question it? For example, if a person realistically feels guilty over the death of someone and decides that celebrating his or her own birthday is no longer appropriate since the dead person will no longer have such special days, is there some reason to question it? Granted, denying oneself a birthday celebration may not be common, but there is no psychological principle that says such celebrations must or should be endured for good mental health. If such an action helps the client cope, then the helper should accept it as reasonable under the circumstances. Assuming there are no psychopathological consequences, whatever works for the person must be judged in light of his or situation, regardless of how it might appear to others, including mental health workers.

FORCING THE ISSUE

It bears repeating that people with real-life problems must not be pressured directly or subtly into confronting issues they choose not to address. Although in the case of a psychopathological disorder such confrontation may be necessary and ultimately beneficial, this is not the case with a real-life problem. The attempt to get the client to acknowledge and deal with thoughts and emotions is based on the assumption that the client is either unaware of them (as if this were possible) or cannot handle them. In fact, the client has come to the realization that discussion, confrontation, and working through really serve no useful purpose and that resolution is not possible. Attempts to coerce a client into discussion are likely to result in an unnecessary and unproductive exacerbation of memories, thoughts, and emotions. Continued efforts, regardless of how well-intentioned the helper, will inevitably result in client withdrawal from treatment.

It is not confrontation and discussion per se that are the problem in this case—it is who initiates them. If the client feels the need to open up, of course the helper should be attentive to that need. However, being realistic about the matter, any helper knows that no one can be forced to talk about anything. Trying to coerce the client will simply produce an uncomfortable situation. It is necessary to reiterate that if a client resists discussion, this must not be interpreted as a sign of defensiveness, resistance, or threat.

TAKING AWAY PROTECTIVE DEFENSES

Under usual therapeutic conditions, it is desirable, indeed, expected that the helper should aim at removal of psychological defense mechanisms. The goal is to help the person see the situation realistically and thereby be able to cope more effectively. In the case of real-life problems, however, the rule changes. If a situation is realistically emotionally overwhelming, using defense mechanisms such as rationalization, compensation, and denial may be the only way to maintain a semblance of normal functioning. For example, referring to survivors of suicide, Rogers, Sheldon, Barwick, Letofsky, and Lancee (1982) stated, "For some, a measure of denial is important, while others feel and express a great deal of guilt and shame" (p. 448).

Although it is true that defense mechanisms take a certain toll in terms of energy and that by definition they involve a degree of self-deception, it must be recognized that real-life situations do not present good options. The person must do the best he or she can in a very difficult situation. If the best option for keeping the person functioning in the best allowable manner is to use defenses, what would be accomplished by trying to take them away?

The important issue for the helper in these circumstances is not that the person is using defenses, but whether they are adaptive or maladaptive. Of course, if defenses create more problems than they help, the issue should be addressed by the helper. Even then, it is debatable whether the goal should be complete removal of the defenses or, what is more likely, minimizing maladaptive effects.

OFFERING UNREALISTIC HOPE

In his or her desire to help a person with a real-life problem, the helper may be tempted to offer hope that is not realistic. There is no guarantee that therapy or any other technique will be able to help a person. There are no guarantees that the passage of time will help or that a change in one's life situation will alleviate anything. Generally, the only realistic hope that can be offered to the person is that someone will be there if she or he feels the need for help. Offering unrealistic hope, regardless of how well intentioned, only serves to further disappoint a person who has already lost a great deal.

USING CLICHES AND PLATITUDES

Therapeutic cliches and platitudes are suitable for wall posters and pop psychology, but they rarely have any use in serious attempts to help a person with a real-life problem. The helper must avoid saying things like "time heals all wounds" to a person who has already suffered for many years and has no reasonable hope that the future holds anything different. Do not say, "You will be a stronger person because of this." How does one respond when the client responds, "Fine, do you want to go through it and become stronger, too?" To say "there is always hope" means nothing to someone who knows better. It is prudent to avoid using phrases like "after the storm comes the calm" when treating a person who knows the storm is not going to end. Every cloud does not have a silver lining, and one should not exhort the client to "keep a positive attitude." Using such platitudes denies the overwhelming nature of the situation and implies there is something positive to be gained from it. Finally, do not offer statements such as, "It's fortunate you have your other children" or "If she had lived, she would have been a vegetable." Regardless of the good intentions of the helper, remarks such as these show a lack of understanding of the person's real-life problems.

MAKING MISGUIDED EXPRESSIONS OF EMPATHY

It is not necessary for a helper to have been through the same situation as a client. One does not have to be (or have been) depressed to help alleviate depression, or to be a substance abuser to help those who abuse drugs. One does not have to be phobic to treat phobias. It is necessary for the helper to have been through a situation if he or she is going to offer statements such as, "I know how you feel" or "I know what you're going through." Unless the helper has actually been through the situation, how could he or she really know what it feels like or what it does to the person? It is more honest and therapeutic for the helper to acknowledge inability to understand the person's anguish and to ask the person to describe that anguish as well as he or she can in words. For people who have been (and are being) buffeted by some severe life situation, it amounts to an intrusion for the helper to claim understanding.

Even if the helper has been through the same situation, he or she cannot completely know what is going on inside the client. Perhaps the only cliche a helper should keep in mind is this: It is impossible to see the world through someone else's eyes. In spite of a common experience, differences in situations and in the personalities assure that no two people can have identical experiences. Even if the helper has been through the same kind of life experience, it is best that he or she acknowledges having a basis for understanding the client, but not to assume commonality of reactions.

GIVING IMPOSSIBLE ADVICE

It may be obvious, but it is important if the client is to continue seeking help that advice be realistic and feasible. Over the years, one of the more common complaints about mental health services has been that the advice given is simply not realistic and cannot be implemented. The recommendations for coping or handling a situation may sound good and may accurately reflect a theoretical position, but it may not be possible for the client to actually follow through with them. For example, it may simply not be possible for a person to get away for awhile, a couple to spend more time alone, a parent to set firm rules for an adolescent, or an employee to confront an abusive employer. It is adequate to offer this kind of advice when a person's situation is conducive to the advice working, but offering advice when situations may not permit its implementation is useless and frustrating for the client. A person may not have the money to get away. A couple may have no one to watch their children so that they can spend time alone.

Further, such advice ignores the fact that if other people are involved, they may choose not to cooperate. Telling a husband to communicate with his wife is helpful only if the wife chooses to communicate with her husband. Advising a woman to stand up to her abusive husband rings hollow when there is a very real chance that if she does so she will be seriously injured or killed. Advising a parent to set firm rules is good advice if the child agrees to abide by them, but what if the child is antisocial and frankly could not care less about the rules and the damage that might come from breaking them? Telling an emotionally drained parent to simply lock the door when a child refuses to obey a curfew ignores the real possibility of an angry son or daughter filing child abuse charges and the parent having to undergo investigation.

Making well-intentioned but unrealistic recommendations to clients leads to two unfortunate consequences. First, such recommendations show with startling clarity how little the helper truly understands about the client's situation. Second, there is the implication that the client is not cooperating with treatment if he or she does not attempt to follow the advice. It is inaccurate to portray a client as resistant when, in fact, she or he is being realistic in determining that trying to implement a recommendation will be futile at best and potentially harmful at worst. If a helper makes such recommendations, it should not be surprising that a client discontinues treatment.

Helpers need to help and are typically trained to expect they will be able to do so. Because of this, the need to deal with real-life problems creates a strong potential for making unrealistic recommendations. After all, both the helper and the client are caught in an overwhelming situation. The helper must thoughtfully consider whether a recommendation can actually be implemented to the advantage of the client. If a helper cannot offer advice, it is more honest and probably more helpful for a helper to admit that he or she has no answers and that he or she is uncertain as to what might help. Certainly, clients should be aware that the helper's recommendations are tentative and, if the effort to follow the helper's advice fails, that failure is not the fault of the client.

EMPLOYING POP PSYCHOLOGY

The term "pop" is short for popular psychology, but although it is popular, many pop psychologists, in fact, are not psychologists. The term is widely used to describe media helpers whose goal is to reach large audiences (radio and television personalities, newspaper columnists, magazine writers, seminars presenters, and some book authors).

Except in the rarest of circumstances, pop psychology cannot be recommended for people undergoing real-life problems. Help offered is meant to appeal to mass audiences and only by chance could some of the advice have direct, specific applicability for a person. Even worse, advice given is naive, cliche and platitude ridden, and so simplistic as to be embarrassing to a serious helper.

Beyond the dubious value of the help they offer, pop psychology sources present another problem. Clients are likely to respond selectively. They will embrace something the "helper" says or writes when they (the clients) are ready to accept it and will reject material they are not yet prepared to face. The greatest concern about such naive self-help sources is that clients will begin to blame themselves when they cannot find meaning in their situation or they simply cannot implement the suggestions offered by the source.

Of course, one must not assume that every advice giver should be categorically rejected simply because his or her work has become popular. The term "well-known" is not necessarily synonymous with the term pop psychology. If a mental health professional chooses to recommend a particular source of help (in this case, it is likely to be a book), it is imperative that she or he be intimately familiar with it and assess its likelihood of offering help to the client. The helper should also help the client by providing guidelines on how to use the source.

EXPECTING A SMOOTH THERAPEUTIC COURSE

Under usual therapeutic conditions, the course of therapy is marked by tentative gains and temporary relapses, but there is a more or less steady progression toward improvement. This is not the case with real-life problems, as Kinzie and Fleck (1987) noted in their work with traumatized refugees. Because there is no resolution in most cases (or it is uncertain in terms of when it might occur, if ever), there is no steady progress toward improvement. With real-life problems there will be periods of relative calm only to have the emotional storm reappear—and the cycle will go on and on. Recurrences of emotional storms are to be expected and do not indicate any failure in the helping process.

Because the types of situations that generate real-life problems leave people emotionally numbed in varying degrees, it is not likely that the helper will receive an outpouring of gratitude for his or her efforts. It is not that the client is unappreciative. Rather, it is simply that the strain is ongoing, and there is no defining moment when the client realizes he or she is on the road to recovery. There will be no moment when the client senses relief from the burden.

Finally, in fairness to helpers in the mental health field, it must be acknowledged that no treatment is perfect and no therapist is perfect. It is unrealistic to expect any therapist always to say the right thing and never to say the wrong thing. Dealing with real-life problems is difficult for the helper, too, especially because the rules of helping are imprecise and ambiguous. Mistakes are unavoidable, but when they occur the helper must acknowledge them and learn from them.

9 THE NEXT STEPS

Two major issues have been directly or indirectly raised in this book and deserve to be addressed in this final chapter. First, what research needs are evident? Second, what suggestions may be offered for professional development?

RESEARCH NEEDS

There is an obvious need for research about real-life problems, both temporal and lasting. Some psychological and emotional conditions which encompass real-life problems have been studied rather extensively, for example, posttraumatic stress disorders and medical illnesses. However, many other real-life problems have not been empirically studied. To name only a few, how many parents or grandparents lives have been devastated by the deprivation of contact with children or grandchildren? How many parents are grieving over a child's life gone wrong? How many people quietly suffer rational guilt? How many people's lives will never be the same for many other reasons? The field must establish prevalence and incidence rates for real-life problems.

Beyond the questions of prevalence and incidence, there is a need to study individual reactions to real-life events. What can we learn from those people who can go through a devastating event with equanimity? Such people do not seek help, but we could learn a great deal from them. What is it about their personalities, experiences, and perceptions that allows them to cope with such strength? Do these people have philosophies about life different from those in which most of us believe? What can we learn from them that would make us better able to help other people undergoing real-life problems? Inversely, is there something we could learn about the backgrounds, personalities, and philosophies of people who do develop real-life problems that would help us identify people who are vulnerable to the effects of real-life problems in general?

Are the differences suggested in this book between temporal and lasting real-life problems warranted? Can any problem of the proportions described here ever be really resolved, or do temporal real-life problems result in lasting effects? Are there lasting effects to all real-life problems and, therefore, is there no need to distinguish between types?

Clearly, there is a need for detailed study of people undergoing all varieties of real-life problems. Are there normal reactions of which we are not yet aware? What kinds of differences might be found in relation to different types of real-life events and their consequences? And, of vital importance, can real-life problems be considered collectively or are there critical differences about which we should know?

How many mental health clients have a real-life problem that has been misdiagnosed as psychopathological? And, especially important, how many people with real-life problems do and do not seek professional intervention? If they do not, why not? A related question is how many people with real-life problems seek help and then drop out of therapy, and why do they drop out. If helping was found to be beneficial, what specifically accounted for the positive results?

Being alert to the need for research is a large step toward addressing it. There is little doubt that mental health researchers will ask other questions about real-life problems and will seek their answers.

PROFESSIONAL DEVELOPMENT

In spite of the lack of empirical data on helping people with real-life problems, there is no doubt that a significant number of people endure them. The mental health field must be prepared to offer help when it is needed.

Helping means more than possessing generalized counseling skills and a caring personality. There is an undeniable need for knowledge about real-life problems. Although undergoing an experience personally is not necessary for one to appreciate the effects of real-life problems, to help another person requires specific knowledge of the situation the person is going through and what is or is not normal. For the present, mental health workers will simply have to search the literature and other resources (e.g., national groups) about her or his client's specific problem.

No individual will ever be able to become an expert in all real-life problems. Sharing among helpers is necessary to disseminate information. There is a need for training seminars and staff discussions about real-life problems. It would be desirable if colleges, universities, and training centers would offer course work on the types of real-life problems this book has addressed. Courses in adjustment or in crisis counseling only touch the surface of these problems.

REFERENCES

Adler, T. (1993, November). Studies look at ways to keep fear at bay. *APA Monitor*, p. 17.

American Psychiatric Association. (1987). *Diagnostic and statistical manual of mental disorders* (3rd ed.-rev.). Washington, DC: Author.

Baekeland, F., & Lundwall, L. (1975). Dropping out of treatment: A critical review. *Psychological Bulletin, 82*, 738-783.

Baider, L., Peretz, T., & DeNour, A. K. (1992). Effect of the Holocaust on coping with cancer. *Social Science and Medicine, 34*, 11-15.

Bergin, A. E., & Jensen, J. P. (1990). Religiosity of psychotherapists: A national survey. *Psychotherapy, 27*, 3-7.

Bernheim, K. F. (1989). Psychologists and families of the severely mentally ill: The role of family consultation. *American Psychologist, 44*, 561-564.

Charmaz, K. (1991). *Good days, bad days: The self in chronic illness and time*. New Brunswick, NJ: Rutgers University Press.

Cohen, L. J., & Roth, S. (1987). The psychological aftermath of rape: Long-term effects and individual differences in recovery. *Journal of Social and Clinical Psychology, 5*, 525-534.

Cohen, S., & Wills, T. A. (1985). Stress, social support, and the buffering hypothesis. *Psychological Bulletin, 98*, 310-357.

Cotton, D. H. (1990). *Stress management: An integrated approach to therapy*. New York: Brunner/Mazel.

Cousins, N. (1979). *Anatomy of an illness*. New York: Norton.

Davidson, J. R. T., & Foa, E. B. (Eds.). (1992). *Posttraumatic stress disorder: DSM IV and beyond.* Washington, DC: American Psychiatric Press.

Davison, G. C., & Neale, J. M. (1994). *Abnormal psychology* (6th ed.). New York: Wiley.

Denton, L. (1993, November). Loftus, Briere draw a crowd to repressed memory debate. *APA Monitor,* p. 5.

Dreman, S. (1989). Children of victims of terrorism in Israel: Coping and adjustment in the face of trauma. *Israel Journal of Psychiatry and Related Sciences, 26,* 212-222.

Eaton, W. W., Signal, J. J., & Weinfield, M. (1982). Impairment in Holocaust survivors after 33 years: Data from an unbiased community sample. *American Journal of Psychiatry, 139,* 773-777.

Everett, F., Proctor, N., & Cartmell, B. (1989). Providing psychological services to American Indian children and families. In D. R. Atkinson, G. R. Morten, & D. W. Sue (Eds.). *Counseling American minorities* (3rd ed.). Dubuque, IA: W. C. Brown.

Everstine, D. S., & Everstine, L. (1993). *The trauma response: Treatment for emotional injury.* New York: Norton.

Fallon, D. (1992). An existential look at B. F. Skinner. *American Psychologist, 47,* 1433-1440.

Finkelstein, H. (1988). The long-term effects of early parent death: A review. *Journal of Clinical Psychology, 44,* 3-9.

Figley, C. R., & McCubbin, H. I. (Eds.). (1983). *Stress and the family: II. Coping with catastrophe.* New York: Brunner/Mazel.

Foy, D. W., Resnick, H. S., & Sipprelle, R. C., & Carrol, E. M. (1987). Premilitary, military, and postmilitary factors in the development of combat-related posttraumatic stress disorder. *The Behavior Therapist, 10,* 3-9.

Gartner, A., & Reissman, F. (1979). *Self-help in the human services.* San Francisco: Jossey-Bass.

Golden, W. L., Gersh, W. D., & Robbins, D. M. (1992). *Psychological treatment of cancer patients: A cognitive-behavioral approach.* Des Moines: Allyn & Bacon.

Gong-Guy, E., Cravens, R. B., & Patterson, T. E. (1991). Clinical issues in mental health service delivery to refugees. *American Psychologist, 46,* 642-648.

Grinker, R. R., Sr., Grinker, R. R., Jr., & Timberlake, J. (1962). "Mentally healthy" young males (homoclites). *Archives of General Psychiatry, 6,* 405-453.

Hatfield, A. B. (1978). Psychological costs of schizophrenia to the family. *Social Work, 23,* 355-359.

Holden, D. F., & Lewine, R. R. J. (1982). How families evaluate mental health professionals, resources and effects of illness. *Schizophrenia Bulletin, 8,* 626-633.

Holmes, C. B. (1992). *Recognizing brain dysfunction: A guide for mental health professionals.* Brandon, VT: Clinical Psychology Publishing Company.

Horowitz, M. J. (1974). Stress response syndromes. *Archives of General Psychiatry, 31,* 768-781.

Jacobs, M. K., & Goodman, G. (1989). Psychology and self-help groups: Predictions on a partnership. *American Psychologist, 44,* 536-545.

Kaminer, W. (1992). *I'm dysfunctional, you're dysfunctional: The recovery movement and other self-help fashions.* Reading, MA: Addison-Wesley.

Katz, A. H. (1981). Self-help and mutual aid: An emerging social movement. *Annual Review of Sociology, 7,* 129-155.

Kelly, G. A. (1955). *The psychology of personal constructs* (2 vols.). New York: Norton.

Kelly, G. A. (1969). The autobiography of a theory. In B. Maher (Ed.). *Clinical psychology and personality: Selected papers of George Kelly.* New York: Wiley.

Kennedy, E. (1981). *Crisis counseling: An essential guide for nonprofessional counselors.* New York: Continuum.

Kinzie, J. D., & Fleck, J. (1987). Psychotherapy with severely traumatized refugees. *American Journal of Psychotherapy, 41,* 82-94.

Kobasa, S. C., Maddi, S. R., & Kahn, S. (1982). Hardiness and health: A prospective study. *Journal of Personality and Social Psychology, 42,* 168-177.

Kubler-Ross, E. (1969). *On death and dying.* New York: Macmillan.

Kurtz, L. F. (1990). The self-help movement: Review of the past decade of research. *Social Work, 13,* 101-115.

Kushner, H. S. (1989). *When bad things happen to good people.* New York: Schocken.

Langer, E. J., & Abelson, R. P. (1974). A patient by any other name . . . : Clinician group difference in labeling bias. *Journal of Consulting and Clinical Psychology, 42,* 4-9.

Lefcourt, H. M., & Martin, R. A. (1986). *Humor and life stress: Antidote to adversity.* New York: Springer-Verlag.

Lerner, A., & Mahlendorf, U. R. (1991). *Life guidance through literature.* Chicago: American Library Association.

Levy, L. H. (1976). Self-help groups: Types and psychological processes. *Journal of Applied Behavioral Science, 12,* 310-322.

Lieberman, M. (1986). Self-help groups and psychiatry. *Psychiatry Update: The American Psychiatric Association Annual Review, 5,* 744-760.

Loftus, E. F. (1993). The reality of repressed memories. *American Psychologist, 48,* 518-537.

Lukas, C., & Seiden, H. M. (1990). *Silent grief: Living in the wake of suicide.* New York: Bantam Books.

Martin, J. A., & Elmer, E. (1992). Battered children grown up: A follow-up study of individuals severely maltreated as children. *Child Abuse and Neglect, 16,* 75-87.

Masson, J. M. (1988). *Against therapy: Emotional tyranny and the myth of psychological healing.* New York: Atheneum.

Masters. R., Friedman, L. N., & Gretzel, G. (1988). Helping families of homicide victims: A multidimensional approach. *Journal of Traumatic Stress, 1,* 109-125.

Mattussek, P. (1975). *Internment in concentration camps and its consequences.* New York: Springer-Verlag.

McCarthy, P. R., Reese, R. G., Schueneman, J. M., & Reese, J. A. (1991). Counseling working class women. *Canadian Journal of Counseling, 25,* 581-593.

McCubbin, H. I., & Figley, C. R. (Eds.). (1983), *Stress and the family: I. Coping with normative transitions.* New York: Brunner/Mazel.

Miller, J. F. (1992). *Coping with chronic illness: Overcoming powerlessness.* Philadelphia: F. A. Davis.

Mollica, R. F. (1988). The trauma story: The psychiatric care of refugee survivors of violence and torture. In F. M. Ochberg (Ed.). *Post-traumatic therapy and victims of violence.* New York: Brunner/Mazel.

Moon, A., & Tashima, N. (1982). *Help seeking behavior and attitudes of Southeast Asian refugees* (NIMH Grant No. 1-R01-MH 32148). San Francisco: Pacific-Asian Mental Health Research Project.

Morreall, J. (1983). *Taking laughter seriously.* Albany: State University of New York.

Murray, H.A. (1951). In nomine diaboli. *The New England Quarterly, 24,* 435-452.

Murstein, B. I., & Fontaine, P. A. (1993). The public's knowledge about psychologists and other mental health professionals. *American Psychologist, 48,* 839-845.

Ness, D. E., & Pfeffer, C. R. (1990). Sequelae of bereavement resulting from suicide. *American Journal of Psychiatry, 147,* 279-285.

Norton, C. S. (1989). *Life metaphors: Stories of ordinary survival.* Carbondale: Southern Illinois University Press.

Offer, D., & Sabshin, M. (1984). *Normality and the life cycle.* New York: Basic Books.

Offer, D., & Sabshin, M. (1966). *Normality: Theoretical and clinical concepts of mental health.* New York: Basic Books.

Offer, D., & Sabshin, M. (1974). *Normality* (rev. ed.). New York: Basic Books.

Offer, D., & Sabshin, M. (Eds.). (1991). *The diversity of normal behavior: Further contributions to normatology.* New York: Basic Books.

Pardek, J. T., & Pardek, J. A. (1992). *Bibliotherapy: A guide to using books in clinical practice.* San Francisco: EMText.

Patel, C. (1991). *The complete guide to stress management.* New York: Plenum.

Peck, M. S. (1978). *The road less travelled.* New York: Simon and Schuster.

Pekarik, G. (1983). Follow-up adjustment of outpatient dropouts. *American Journal of Orthopsychiatry, 53,* 501-511.

Pekarik, G. (1985). Coping with dropouts. *Professional Psychology: Research & Practice, 16,* 114-123.

Peper, E., & Holt, C. F. (1992). *Creating wholeness: A self-healing workbook using dynamic relaxation, images, and thoughts.* New York: Plenum.

Phillips, H. C. (1988). *Psychological management of chronic pain: A treatment manual.* New York: Springer.

Potter-Effron, R. T. (1987). Shame and guilt: Definitions, processes and treatment with AODA clients. *Alcoholism Treatment Quarterly, 4,* 7-24.

Powell, T. J. (1987). *Self-help organizations and professional practice.* Silver Springs, MD: National Association of Social Workers.

Rando, T. A. (1986). *Parental loss of a child.* Champaign, IL: Research Press.

Rappaport, J., Seidman, E., Toro, P. A., McFadden, L. S., Reischl, T. M., Roberts, L. J., Salem, D.A., Stein, C. H., & Zimmerman, M. A. (1985, Winter). Collaborative research with a mutual help organization. *Social Policy, 50,* 12-24.

Reissman, F. (1985, Winter). New dimensions in self-help. *Social Policy, 50,* 2-5.

Rogers, J., Sheldon, A., Barwick, C., Letofsky, K., & Lancee. W. (1982). Help for families of suicide: Survivors support program. *Canadian Journal of Psychiatry, 27,* 444-449.

Rosenhan, D. L. (1973). On being sane in insane places. *Science, 179,* 250-258.

Rynearson, E. K. (1981). Suicide internalized: An existential sequestrum. *American Journal of Psychiatry, 138*, 84-87.

Sargent, J., & Lieberman, R. (1985). Childhood chronic illness: Issues for psychotherapists. *Community Mental Health Journal, 21*, 294-311.

Shakespeare, W. (1982). *The complete works of William Shakespeare.* Minneapolis, MN: Amaranth Press.

Smith, D. (1982). Trends in counseling and psychotherapy. *American Psychologist, 37*, 802-809.

Smith, J. C. (1986). *Meditation: A sensible guide to a timeless discipline.* Champaign, IL: Research Press.

Smith, M. L., Glass, G. V., & Miller, T. J. (1980). *The benefits of psychotherapy.* Baltimore: Johns Hopkins.

Stahler, G. J., & Eisenman, R. (1987). Psychotherapy dropouts: Do they have poor psychological adjustment? *Bulletin of the Psychonomic Society, 25*, 198-200.

Sue, D. W., & Sue, D. (1992). *Counseling the culturally different* (2nd ed.). New York: Wiley.

Sulloway, F. (1991). Reassessing Freud's case histories: The social construction of psychoanalysis. *ISIS, 82*, 245-275.

Tavris, C. (1992). *The mismeasure of woman.* New York: Simon and Schuster.

Tavris. C. (1993, January 3). Beware the incest-survivor machine. *New York Times*, pp. 1, 16-17.

Tyler, L. E. (1980). The next twenty years. *The Counseling Psychologist, 8*, 19-21.

van der Veer, G. (1992). *Counseling and therapy with refugees: Psychological problems of victims of war, torture and repression.* New York: Wiley.

Werth, L. H., & Oseroff, A. B. (1987) Continual counseling intervention: Lifetime support for the family with a handicapped member. *American Journal of Family Therapy, 15*, 333-342.

Westermeyer, J. (1987). Cultural factors in clinical assessment. *Journal of Consulting and Clinical Psychology. 55*, 471-478.

White, R. W. (1964). *The abnormal personality.* New York: Ronald Press.

Wholey, D. (1992). *When the worst that can happen already has: Conquering life's most difficult times.* New York: Hyperion.

Wolman, B. B. (Ed.). (1976). *The therapist's handbook: Treatment methods of mental disorders.* New York: Van Nostrand Reinhold Company.

Ziv, A. (1984). *Personality and sense of humor.* New York: Springer.

INDEX